Self-Working
CLOSE-UP
CARD MAGIC

56 Foolproof Tricks

by KARL FULVES

With 119 Illustrations by
JOSEPH K. SCHMIDT

DOVER PUBLICATIONS, INC.
NEW YORK

Copyright

Copyright © 1995 by Karl Fulves.
All rights reserved under Pan American and International Copyright Conventions.

Published in Canada by General Publishing Company, Ltd., 30 Lesmill Road, Don Mills, Toronto, Ontario.
Published in the United Kingdom by Constable and Company, Ltd., 3 The Lanchesters, 162–164 Fulham Palace Road, London W6 9ER.

Bibliographical Note

Self-Working Close-Up Card Magic: 56 Foolproof Tricks is a new work, first published by Dover Publications, Inc., in 1995.

Library of Congress Cataloging-in-Publication Data

Fulves, Karl.
    Self-working close-up card magic: 56 foolproof tricks / by Karl Fulves; with 119 illustrations by Joseph K. Schmidt.
        p.   cm.
    ISBN 0-486-28124-8 (pbk.)
    1. Card tricks. I. Schmidt, Joseph K. II. Title.
GV1549.F85 1995
795.4'38—dc20
                                                            94-16898
                                                            CIP

Manufactured in the United States of America
Dover Publications, Inc.,
31 East 2nd Street,
Mineola, N.Y. 11501

INTRODUCTION

For the person who has decided to take up magic, close-up card magic is an excellent hobby. You can have fun even as you learn your craft. Playing cards are inexpensive and are available in many homes. The magician who performs close-up card magic can entertain at parties and family get-togethers. Unlike the stage magician, who requires special apparatus, lighting, music and a large auditorium in which to practice his craft, the close-up magician is ready at a moment's notice whenever a deck of cards is handy.

Close-up card magic is performed right under the noses of the spectators. It has an immediacy that cannot be duplicated by platform magic. Seasoned professionals agree there is no better way to learn how to handle an audience than when it is inches away.

It is a good idea to try each trick in this book to see which ones suit your style of performance. Pick one trick from each of three or four different chapters, routine them together, and you will have a short card act that can be performed any time for friends and family.

I would like to thank Joseph K. Schmidt for the artwork that makes these tricks so easy to follow.

KARL FULVES

CONTENTS

OPENERS

The opening card trick has a special requirement attached to it. The opening trick should have a simple plot because that is the best way to engage the audience's attention. The tricks in this chapter have strong, simple plots that set the stage for the other tricks you will perform.

1. Magic by Design

In this routine the cards are animated to produce a duplicate of a chosen design. A variety of designs are shown on a list, Figure 1. The spectator picks a card from the deck. He is told that if the card is an ace, he would choose design No. 1, the straight line; that if he picks a 2, his design would be No. 2, crossed lines. The card he picks is the 3. This means that he picked design No. 3, the triangle.

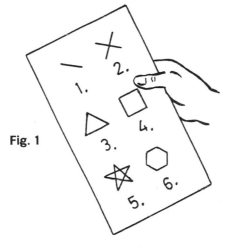

Fig. 1

The deck is cut and the two halves placed on the card case. A rubber band is snapped around the apparatus, Figure 2. The magician releases the cards. Instantly they form themselves into a triangle, Figure 3, thus duplicating the chosen design.

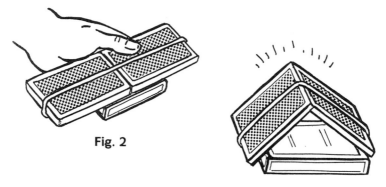

Fig. 2

Fig. 3

Method: This impromptu routine is based on Aldo Colombini's handling of a popular effect. It can be done with any borrowed deck. Draw the list of designs shown in Figure 1 on a large sheet of paper. Have a rubber band handy.

Hold the deck so the faces of the cards are toward you. Spread the cards until you find a 3. Cut the deck and complete the cut so the 3 is brought to the top of the deck. Remove seven cards from the deck. These cards are a mixture of aces, 2's, 4's, 5's and 6's. Suits are not important. Briefly show the faces of these cards. Hand them to the spectator. Ask him to mix them and drop them on top of the deck.

Show the diagram of Figure 1. Explain that the spectator is going to choose a card that will indicate one of the designs. Since there are six designs, you will use the cards with values from 1 to 6 for the random selection of a number. Tell him that if the card he picks is a 6, for example, you will use the design with six sides (the hexagon). If he picks the 5, you will use the five-pointed star, and so on.

Deal the top eight cards off the deck one at a time into a heap on the table. Say that you will arrive at a random number by an elimination shuffle. In magician's parlance, the shuffle is known as a down-under or duck-and-deal shuffle. Remove the top card of the packet and put it under the packet. Remove the new top card and put it on the table. Put the new top card under the packet, the next card onto the table, and so on, until you have one card left.

Say, "The value of this card will tell us the design you chose." Do not show the face of the card yet. Place the card on the table face down.

Cut the deck in half. Place each half on the card case. Hold the apparatus in place while you snap a rubber band around it, Figure 2. Turn up the playing card. It will be the 3.

Say, "You chose a 3. That means you picked the triangle. Watch."

Release the apparatus. The cards will automatically arrange themselves into the triangular shape shown in Figure 3, thus correctly matching the shape chosen by the spectator.

2. True Colors

Face-up and face-down cards are mixed together. It looks like a hopeless muddle, but red cards sort themselves from blacks, and there is a surprise finish.

Method: This clever routine is based on ideas of Bill Simon and John Scarne. The effect is out of proportion to the modest amount of prior presentation. Place all the red cards on top of the deck, all the black cards on the bottom. Leave the deck in the case until the time of performance.

To present the routine, remove the deck from the case. Cut it between the colors so that all red cards are in one group, all black cards in the other. Place the black heap on the table. Spread the red cards face down. Push six or seven cards out of this packet and hand them to a spectator. Ask him to take one card from this packet, turn it face up and insert it into the middle of the face-down packet.

Spread the black half of the deck face down. Push six or seven cards out of this packet. Hand these cards to a second spectator. Have him remove one card, turn it face up and insert it into the center of the small packet.

At this point each spectator holds a small face-down packet with a face-up card in it. Turn the small red packet face up.

Dovetail or riffle shuffle it into the large black packet. Turn the small black packet face up. Similarly shuffle it into the large red packet. Then, to really mix the cards, turn the large red packet face up and riffle shuffle it into the face-down black packet.

Say, "The cards are really mixed up. But if we give them a shake, they will sort themselves out." Snap the fingers. Spread the deck so the red side is face up. All of the face-up cards are red. This will come as a surprise to the audience. The second surprise is that there is one black card in the packet. Slide the black card out. As you do, say, "All the face-up cards are red except one black card, and that is the card you chose, sir."

Flip the deck over. Spread it on the table. All of the face-up cards are black except one card. Say, "And all of these cards are black except one card, and that is the card this other gentleman chose."

The two ways of performing this type of shuffle are shown in Figure 4. The dovetail shuffle is performed with the hands holding the ends of the packets. The corner riffle is performed with the hands holding the sides of the packets. The corner riffle is better for this trick because the cards are held low to the table. Hence you are better able to conceal the fact that the face-up packet contains cards of one color.

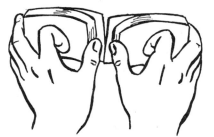

Fig. 4   Dovetail

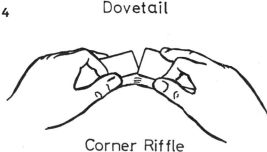

Corner Riffle

3. Flyaway Cards

The disappearance of a playing card is always a mysterious feat. In this trick two freely chosen cards vanish from the deck and are later found reversed in the center of the deck. A borrowed pack may be used.

Method: Hold the deck face up. Ask the spectator to name two cards. Say he names the red jacks. Spread the cards, remove the red jacks and place them on the face of the deck.

Say, "This is a terrific way to make your two cards vanish." Place the deck behind your back. When the deck is out of sight, turn it face down. Deal off the top four cards, turn them over and replace them on top of the deck. Then turn the deck face up again. Deal off the two face cards (the chosen cards). Keep them face up as you place them at the back of the deck. The situation now is that you have the face-up deck, then four face-down cards, then the two face-up chosen cards.

Bring the deck into view. Say, "See, your two cards have vanished. It's an amazing trick!" The audience will think you are kidding. Push the four face cards of the deck to the right. Turn the right hand palm down and take these four cards. The fingers are on the faces of the cards, the thumb in back. Say, "No jacks." Turn the cards face down and place them under the deck.

Continue with the remainder of the face-up cards. Each time show four or five cards, turn them face down and place them under the deck. When you run out of face-up cards, say, "Your two cards have vanished."

Place the deck face down on the table. Cut the deck and complete the cut. As you do, say, "You probably guessed that I put your two cards in my back pocket." Reach into the back pocket. Pretend to have trouble removing the two cards. Of course the pocket is empty so it is all a matter of acting. Bring out the two imaginary cards and pretend to toss them onto the deck. Slap the top of the deck with the other hand.

Spread the deck face down on the table. Up to now the audience will have thought it is all a joke, so it will be surprised to see the two chosen cards face up in the middle of the deck.

4. Too Many Cards

The magician explains what happens when he is dealt too many cards in a game of gin rummy. He causes the cards to travel mysteriously back to the other player's hand.

Method: Secretly place two cards in your jacket pocket prior to performance. This is the only preparation, but it sets up a baffling double mystery.

Deal five cards off the top of the deck into a face-up heap, saying, "Ten, nine, eight, seven, six." Then deal four cards into a separate heap as you say, "One, two, three, four."

Place one heap on top of the other. "Six and four are ten. That's how many cards are dealt to each player in a game of gin rummy. Please place these ten cards in your pocket for the moment."

Repeat the above procedure, apparently to count a packet of six and a packet of four cards. Put one packet on top of the other. Say, "Four and six are ten. This is my gin-rummy hand."

Place the deck on the table. Hold the packet in the left hand. Say, "Gamblers sometimes cheat and add a card to their hand. Give me the top card of your hand."

Place the spectator's card on top of your gin-rummy hand. "Now I have 11 cards. Of course I would never cheat in a game, so I'd get rid of this card. This is how it's done." Give your packet a shake. Then deal your cards one at a time onto the table, counting aloud as you deal. You have ten cards. It looks as if one card vanished from your hand.

Hand the spectator two cards. Ask him to add them to his gin-rummy hand. Then place your gin hand into the pocket where you have the extra two cards concealed.

Say, "Now you have 12 cards. Please remove your gin hand." When the spectator has brought his packet out of his pocket, say, "Give them a shake." After he has given the packet a shake, say, "Now you have 11 cards. Give them another shake."

When he has done this, say, "Good. You have ten cards again. Count them on the table." The spectator counts his cards. He does indeed have ten cards. Remove your packet, including the two extra cards. Count them to show that you too have ten cards. Say, "A hand of rummy, anyone?"

5. Caught Between

George Delaney invented a baffling trick in which a chosen card is caught between two reversed cards. The secret is offbeat and will even fool magicians.

Method: Spread the deck face down between the hands. Invite the spectator to remove five cards from different parts of the deck. Say, "I want you to pick a card, but I don't want to influence your choice." Turn your back so you cannot see his cards. Say to him, "Discard two of the five cards." When he has done this, say, "Three are left. Pick one of the three cards as your chosen card."

The real reason for turning your back is so you can do the secret work. You are holding the face-down deck in your hand. Turn the top card face up on top of the deck. Then turn the entire deck over. Turn the face card of the deck face down onto the deck. Because of the two reversed cards, it appears as if the deck is face down. Only the top and bottom cards are really face down, however. The rest of the deck is face up.

Turn and face the audience. Say, "Which card did you choose?" Whatever card the spectator indicates, turn that card face up on the table. Drop the supposed face-down deck on top of the chosen card. Pick up the deck and place it in the left hand.

"I'm going to send your card into the fourth dimension." Grasp the front of the deck as shown in Figure 5. Turn the deck

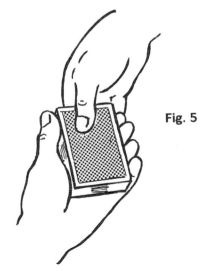

Fig. 5

over and place it back into the left hand, Figure 6. Turn the left hand palm down. Grasp the near end of the deck as shown in Figure 7. While the right hand holds the deck, the left hand turns palm up. The right hand then turns the deck over and places it into the left hand. The audience does not know it, but you have succeeded in turning the deck face down.

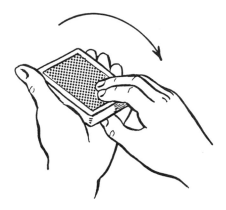

Fig. 6

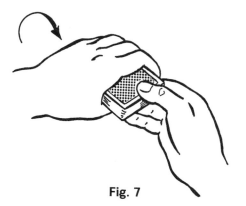

Fig. 7

Say, "We'll cut your card into the middle of the pack." Cut off the top half of the deck with the right hand and place it on the table. Then grasp the other half of the deck from above with the right hand, Figure 8. Turn the packet over. Point to the bottom card, Figure 9, as you say, "Here's your card." Turn the right hand palm down and place the packet on top of the other cards.

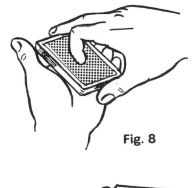

Fig. 8

Fig. 9

Say, "First I'll cause your card to turn face down." Snap the fingers over the deck. "Then I'll cause two other cards to turn face up." Snap the fingers again. "Now I'll put your card between those two cards." Snap the fingers one more time.

Spread the deck face down on the table. There are two reversed cards in the center of the deck and the chosen card is face down between them.

Theodore Annemann suggested a subtle angle. Before performing the trick, look through the cards on the excuse that you want to make sure they are well mixed. Remember the top and bottom card. Say these are the red aces. At the end of the Delaney trick, when the chosen card has been cut into the middle of the deck, say, "I'm going to cause a red ace to turn face up." Snap the fingers. Say, "Done. Now the other red ace." Snap the fingers again. "Good. Now the hard part. I'm going to cause your card to turn over and transport itself to a position between the reversed aces." Snap the fingers, spread the deck and show the result.

6. Perplexing Pen

A spectator picks any card, signs his name on it and buries it in a packet. The packet is mixed and placed on top of the deck. The pen used by the spectator finds the card in a surprising way.

Method: Apart from the deck of cards, you will need a pen with a clip on it. Some pens work more smoothly than others, so you may wish to experiment with different styles of pen.

While you turn your head aside, ask a spectator to deal two equal packets onto the table. It does not matter how many cards are dealt, as long as each packet contains the same number of cards. The spectator looks at the top card of either packet, signs his name on it with the pen and replaces it on top of the other packet. He then places the smaller packet on top of all.

Pick up the combined packet. Remark that you will mix the cards. The left hand grasps the packet from above. The right hand draws the top and bottom card off together, Figure 10. This pair of cards is placed on top of the deck. Continue in the same way with all the remaining cards, drawing pairs of cards off and placing them on top of the deck. Unknown to the audience, the signed card is now on top of the deck.

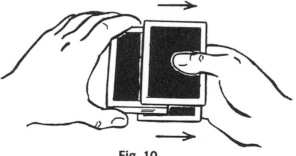

Fig. 10

Say, "The pen will try to seek out the card you wrote on. This should be easy because there is only one card in the deck with ink from this pen on it."

Grasp the deck from above by the ends with the left hand. The left first finger pulls back the top card, causing it to buckle or curve away from the deck as shown in Figure 11. The audience does not see this because the face of the deck is toward it.

Slide the pen up between the deck and the top card, Figure 12. To the audience it appears as if you are stabbing the pen into the middle of the deck.

Engage the top card in the clip. Then slide the pen down and away from the deck, Figure 13. The pen has caught the signed card. This novel trick was suggested by the Swedish magician El Duco.

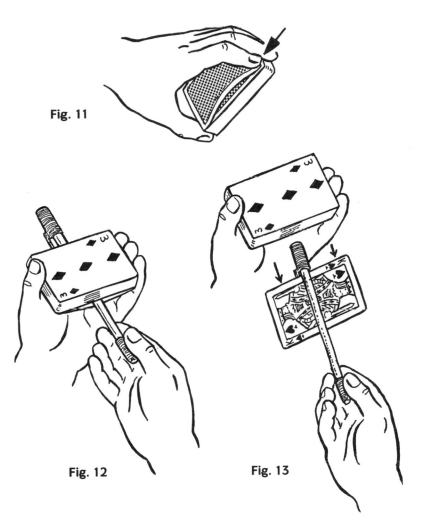

Fig. 11

Fig. 12

Fig. 13

7. The Almanac Deck

By means of an entertaining story, the magician finds a chosen card. The trick is impromptu and can be done with a borrowed deck of cards.

Method: This is the author's presentation for a classic trick known as "The Soldier's Almanac." When you get the borrowed deck, say, "Every deck of cards is programmed with information about the passage of time. First I have to determine if this deck is on Eastern Standard or Daylight Saving Time."

Place the deck behind your back. Take the top face-down card, turn it face up and place it on the bottom of the deck. Deal off the new top card, keep it face down and place it on the bottom of the deck. The reversed card is now second from the bottom.

Bring the deck into view. Spread the top half. Ask a spectator to remove a card and look at it. Square up the deck, taking care not to expose the reversed card. Have the chosen card replaced on top. Then cut the deck and complete the cut.

Say, "When I put the deck behind my back, I reversed a card. Let's see what it is." Spread the cards until you get to the reversed card. Cut the deck at that point and complete the cut so the reversed card is on top. Say, "This card is red, indicating that your deck is on Daylight Saving Time." It does not matter whether the reversed card is red or black; *always* say the deck is on Daylight Saving Time. Deal this face-up card off to the right on the table. Say, "We'll get back to it in a moment."

Continue, "Here's what I mean about every deck being programmed about the passage of time. There are 12 picture cards in the deck, corresponding to the 12 months of the year." Deal a heap of 12 cards onto the table, dealing the cards one at a time off the top of the deck. Pick up the heap and replace it on top of the deck.

Then say, "There are 52 cards in the deck, corresponding to the 52 weeks of the year." Deal a heap of five cards onto the table. Then deal a separate heap of two cards. Pick up the 5-card heap, place it on top of the two-card heap, then place the combined heap on top of the deck.

Say, "Finally, if you add the values of all the cards in the deck, plus one for the joker, we get 365, exactly matching the

365 days of the year." Deal a heap of three cards. Next to it deal a heap of six cards. Next to that deal a heap of five cards. Place the three-card heap on top of the six-card heap. Place this combined heap on top of the five-card heap. Then place this heap on top of the deck.

Say, "And speaking of time, it's time to find your card." Pick up the face-up card you placed aside earlier. Turn it face down and place it on top of the deck. "This card indicated that the deck is on Daylight Saving Time." Spell D-A-Y-L-I-G-H-T, dealing a card for each letter into a heap. Then spell S-A-V-I-N-G, dealing a card for each letter. Say, "What was your card?" When the chosen card is named, turn up the last card dealt—it will be the chosen card.

8. Ace Finds Ace

The spectator shuffles a deck of cards, cuts the deck into two packets, and places the packets in the performer's hands. The performer places the two halves of the deck under the table. The spectator removes a card from one half of the deck, turns it over and inserts it into the other half of the deck.

The deck is reassembled and handed directly to the spectator. He spreads the deck face down on the table. The face-up card is a black ace. The card right next to it proves to be the other black ace.

The trick may be repeated. In this case the spectator discovers that he chose a red ace, and when he inserted the ace into the deck, it found the other red ace. This trick is based on ideas of Joseph Dunninger and John Scarne, two of the top professionals in magic.

Method: Beforehand, remove the black aces from the deck. Place them back to back and conceal them in the left jacket sleeve. The two hidden cards may be held more securely if a rubber band is circled around the wrist and the two cards tucked under the rubber band.

To present the routine, have the spectator shuffle the deck. Instruct him to cut off the top half, take it under the table and place it into your left hand. Request that he give the remaining half of the deck a thorough mixing. While he does this, silently remove the two aces from the sleeve and place them on top of the packet in the left hand. Then turn the entire packet over. Place the face-up packet back into the left hand. So as to better conceal action from audience view, lean slightly forward in your chair and press your forearms against the table. The arms thus remain motionless while the hands perform the concealed action.

When the spectator has mixed the other half of the deck, have him put this packet into the right hand. Remark that since the cards are out of sight, his selection of a card will be truly random. Invite him to remove a card from the packet in your right hand, turn it over and insert it into the packet in your left hand.

When he has done this, turn the left-hand packet over and place this packet under the right-hand packet. Ask him to take the deck from you and spread it face down on the table.

There will be a face-up card in the deck. Remark, "You picked a black ace. Wouldn't it be amazing if you placed it right next to the other black ace?" Have him remove the card under the black ace. It will be the other black ace.

If you plan to repeat the trick, place the red aces back to back and conceal them in the right jacket sleeve. When you are asked to do the trick again, you are all set to produce the other two aces.

CRIME DOES NOT PAY

Since the gangster movie has become a popular form of entertainment, it pays to weave detective or gangster themes into card tricks. If you can tell a good story, card tricks built around such themes have many possibilities for solid entertainment. Use names from news stories about mobsters to keep the patter up to date. The plot ideas in this chapter all carry the message that crime does not pay.

9. The Three Burglars

The magician tells the story of the three burglars who broke into a bank in search of a rare coin. An alert detective saved the day with a little help from his friends.

Method: This is an updated version of a classic trick. Beforehand, remove two kings from the deck. Place a red jack between them. Put these three cards on the bottom of the deck. In addition to the deck of cards, you will need a coin such as a nickel or quarter.

To perform the trick, explain that three burglars heard that a rare coin was going to be stored in a local bank. As you speak, remove three jacks and a king from the deck. These cards are not part of the setup on the bottom of the deck.

Place the deck face down on the table. Explain that the jacks represent three burglars. The king is a detective. Place the coin on top of the deck. Remark that the burglars heard that the bank was keeping a rare coin locked in its vault and that the thieves planned to steal the coin.

Turn the jacks face down. Place one of the black jacks on the bottom of the deck. As you do, say, "One of the burglars went into the basement of the bank." Slide the red jack into the center of the deck. Hold the deck and coin as shown in Figure 14 to steady the apparatus as the card is placed into the deck. Say, "One burglar went in the front door."

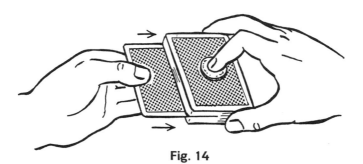

Fig. 14

Place the other black jack on top of the deck. "And one burglar went in from the roof." Show the king and place it on top of the deck. "A detective was walking by and saw the break-in. He went after the burglars."

Cut the deck at about the center and complete the cut. "Knowing that the detective was after them, the burglars tried to escape." Now cut the deck again, but this time cut it at the coin and complete the cut so the coin is back on the top of the deck.

"The rare coin was saved by quick police work." Place the coin on the table. Turn the deck face up. "The burglars were arrested by the detective, with a little help from his friends."

As you speak, deal the face card off onto the table. It will be a jack. Deal the next card onto it. It will be a king. In a similar way deal the next four cards to the table, showing that the three burglars were captured by three detectives.

10. Bonnie and Clyde

Bonnie and Clyde were bank robbers who eluded arrest until they were picked out of a lineup by witnesses. This trick is an amusing demonstration of how easy it is to pick the culprits out of a police lineup.

Method: Remove the four queens from the deck, saying that one of these cards will be picked to represent Bonnie. Then put the four kings in a separate heap, saying that one of the kings will play the part of Clyde. Also remove the ♠A from the deck. This represents Sam Spade, the detective who solved the case.

Shuffle the queens. Have the spectator pick one to play the part of Bonnie. Place this queen face down on the table. Drop the rest of the queen packet on top of this card.

Shuffle the kings. Have the spectator pick one to represent Clyde. Place this king face down on the table. Drop the rest of the king packet on top of it. The names of the two chosen cards can be jotted down on a slip of paper.

Place the king packet on top of the queen packet. Turn the ♠A face up and place it on top of all. Say, "After they robbed a bank, Bonnie and Clyde would lose themselves in the crowd. This time they were followed by Sam Spade." Draw the top and bottom card off the packet. Place this pair of cards on the table. Draw off the next pair in the same way and place it on top of the tabled pair. Continue in this way with all the cards in the packet. This method of mixing cards is known as the milk-build shuffle. It is illustrated in Figure 10.

Pick up the packet and deal it into two heaps. The first card goes into one heap. The second card goes into a separate heap. The next card goes into the first heap, the next into the second heap, and so on until all of the cards have been dealt. When you get to the face-up ♠A, place it to one side.

Say, "Sam Spade arrested several people and had them appear in a police lineup. You can see how easy it is to pick out the culprits." Pick up the king packet. Deal the three kings face up from the bottom of the packet onto the table. Then deal the last card. It will be the only queen in the packet, and further, it will be the card chosen to represent Bonnie.

Deal the cards from the other packet in a separate face-up row. There will be three queens and one king, and the king will be the card that was chosen to play the part of Clyde. Say, "It's easy to pick the guilty party out of the lineup."

11. Go to Jail

The spectator picks two cards to play the part of thieves. One is found by a detective card. The other disappears from the deck and is found between two other detective cards inside the card case.

Method: This trick is based on ideas of Stewart James and the author. Preparation consists of leaving one card inside the card case when you remove the deck. When you are ready to perform the trick, have the deck shuffled and cut.

Ask a spectator to name a number between 1 and 10. He counts that number of cards off the top of the deck into a heap, looks at the top card of the heap, signs his name on it, and puts the card on top of the deck. Then he places the counted heap on top of the deck.

A second spectator picks a number between 10 and 20. He counts that number of cards into a heap, signs his name on the top card, places the signed card on top of the deck, and then places the heap on top of the deck.

Assume the two numbers were 6 and 15. Say, "When the crime was committed, a bystander noticed two digits on the license place of the getaway car." Name the number that is the difference between the two numbers. In our example, the difference between 6 and 15 is 9. Deal that number of cards into a heap on the table. We will call this heap *A*.

The other number is one less than the first spectator's number. In our example, one less than 6 is 5. "The other number the witness saw was 5." Deal that number of cards into a separate heap on the table. We will call this heap *B*.

Pick up the top card of heap *A*. Put the top card of heap *B* on top of this. Place the two cards inside the card case on top of the card that is concealed there. "Two detectives went back to the police station."

Gather the cards in heaps *A* and *B*. Give them a quick shuffle. Invite a spectator to pick a card from the deck. "Another detective was called in on the case." The card chosen by the spectator is turned face up and placed on top of the deck. Put the combined cards from *A* and *B* on top of the deck. Ask the spectator to cut the deck and complete the cut.

"Quick police work solved the case." Spread the deck face down on the table. Remove the face-up card and the card that lies just below it. Turn this card over. It is one of the culprits.

Spread the deck face up on the table. "The other fellow escaped the police roadblock, but he was captured and brought to jail."

Remove the three cards from the card case without disturbing their order. Turn up each of the end cards. Say, "These are the detectives." Then turn up the center card. "And here's the other culprit."

One way to make sure that only one card stays behind inside the card case is to jog the top card of the deck so it protrudes about a half-inch from the case as shown in Figure 15. Leave the cased deck lying on its side in your jacket pocket until you are ready to perform. When you want to do a few card tricks, remove the deck. Hold it in the left hand. The first finger of the right hand slides between the jogged card and the balance of the deck. The first finger and thumb then pull the deck out of the case, Figure 16, leaving the single card in the case.

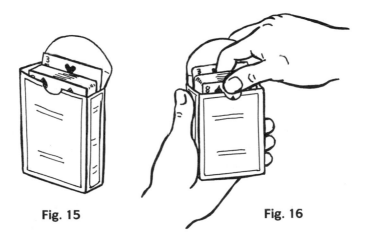

Fig. 15   **Fig. 16**

Even easier is this method: The spectator can remove the deck from the case. Drop the empty case in your jacket pocket. When ready to perform "Go to Jail," remark that you will need the card case for this trick. Reach into the pocket and remove a duplicate card case that already has one card in it.

12. Pack of Lies

In this ingenious mystery, the detective deduces which one of six suspects stole a priceless diamond. The trick is impromptu and can be done any time you are with several friends. It is based on ideas of Keith Downs and Jack Yates.

Method: Remove three low-value red cards and three black picture cards from the deck. While you turn your back, ask someone to shuffle these six cards and distribute one to each of six people. Explain that those who drew the red cards will play the part of people who always tell the truth, even under duress. Those who drew the picture cards will play the part of people who always lie, even under oath.

Remove the ◆A from the deck and place it on the table. Explain that it represents the Hope Diamond, a gem worth millions. While you turn your back, one of the six spectators places the ◆A in his pocket. This person represents the thief who stole the Hope Diamond.

Turn and face the spectators. "Six suspects were called in for questioning." As you speak, write down their names on a sheet of paper. Ask each person if he or she stole the Hope Diamond. The truth tellers must tell the truth. The liars must lie. Record each person's answer on the pad. The answers might look like

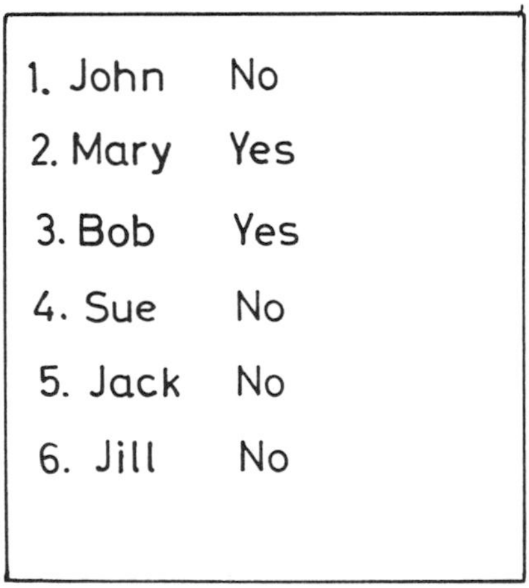

1.	John	No
2.	Mary	Yes
3.	Bob	Yes
4.	Sue	No
5.	Jack	No
6.	Jill	No

Fig. 17

those shown in Figure 17. Since you do not know who is telling the truth, these answers do not tell you who the culprit is.

You will get either two "no" and four "yes" answers, or two "yes" and four "no" answers. Pretend that the culprit is probably one of the two people who gave the same answer. In our example they are Mary and Bob. Ask the other four spectators if Bob did it. Ask Bob if Mary did it. Ask Mary if Bob did it. Record the answers next to the first answers on the pad. The result may look as shown in Figure 18.

1. John	No	Yes ←
2. Mary	Yes	Yes
3. Bob	Yes	Yes
4. Sue	No	No
5. Jack	No	No
6. Jill	No	No

Fig. 18

Five of the spectators will answer the second question the same way they did the first. One person will answer the second question opposite to the way he answered the first question. In the example shown in Figure 18, that person is John. He is the culprit.

Say something like, "I was told that when the culprit ran from the scene of the crime, he was wearing a white shirt, blue trousers and a gold watch." Here you simply describe the person you know to be the culprit. Point to him and say, "Sir, you are under arrest!"

MEMORY TRICKS

A good card memory has many benefits to the card player. Gamblers will tell you that the player who can remember which cards have been played has a strong advantage in such games as blackjack, rummy and bridge. It follows that memory tricks are popular with audiences young and old. In this chapter the magician demonstrates an apparently uncanny ability to memorize cards.

13. Super Count

Card counters are reputed to be able to memorize all of the cards that have been played at blackjack. Their methods actually rely on different techniques. This demonstration looks like the real thing. The ♦A through ♦10 are removed from the deck. The spectator hides one of these cards. The rest of the packet is shuffled and cut. The magician deals the cards face up onto the table. As soon as he deals the last card, he says, "I didn't see the ♦8. Is that the missing card?" The spectator produces the missing card. It is the ♦8. The trick may be repeated.

Method: It appears as if you have the ability to deal quickly through nine cards and immediately name the card you did not see. The method is actually much easier.

If you add the values of the ace, 2, 3 and so on up to 10, the total will be 55.

When the spectator removes a card, the total is less than 55. The difference between 55 and the new total is the value of the missing card.

The handling is as follows. Remove the ♦A through ♦10 from the deck. Ask the spectator to mix the cards, remove one card, sight unseen, and place it in his pocket. He mixes the remaining cards and gives them to you. Hold the packet face down in the left hand.

Deal the cards one at a time into a face-up heap. As you do, silently add together the values of the cards. If the first card is a 4 and the next a 7, the total of the first two cards is 11. If the next card is an 8, the new total is 19. Continue adding the values until you have totaled all nine cards.

The total may be 50. Subtract this from 55 to get a result of 5. Say, "The only card I didn't see is the ♦5." The spectator removes the card from his pocket and it is the ♦5.

The principle can be disguised if the suits are mixed. Use the ♦A, ♦3 and ♦5; the ♣2, ♣4 and ♣6; the ♠7 and ♠9; and the ♥8 and ♥10. When these ten cards are mixed together, they appear to be a random group of cards. The handling of the trick is otherwise the same. If you commit the suits to memory, you can reveal the value and suit of the missing card.

14. Mental Countdown

Taking a shuffled deck from the audience, the magician memorizes the cards. He spreads the deck face up on the table and says, "Point to any card." Say someone points to the ♣4. The magician closes up the spread, does a mental countdown and says, "The ♣4 is the twentieth card in the deck." He counts to the twentieth card and it is the ♣4. The trick may be repeated several times.

Method: Beforehand, place the ♣7 tenth from the top of the deck, the ♥7 twentieth from the top, and ♠7 thirtieth from the top and the ♦7 fortieth from the top. Remember the suit order of the 7's. One mnemonic is the word *CHaSeD*. The uppercase letters give the proper suit rotation. Another memory aid is to recall the initial letter in each word of the sentence, "*Can He Save Dollars.*" CHSD stands for the correct suit order, clubs–hearts–spades–diamonds.

A strong feature of this demonstration is that the deck is genuinely shuffled. Hand the top ten cards to one spectator, the next ten to another spectator and so on. The last spectator gets the final 12 cards of the deck. Each shuffles his cards.

Take back the packet that contains the ♣7. Thumb cards into the right hand as shown in Figure 19. When you get to the ♣7, fan the cards in the left hand, glance at them, then place the left-hand cards onto the right-hand packet, Figure 20. The ♣7 is now tenth from the top.

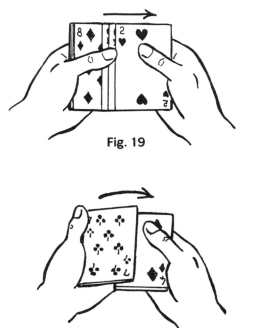

Fig. 19

Fig. 20

Take the packet that contains the ♥7. Handle it the same way you did the ♣7 packet. Follow the same procedure with the ♠7 packet and the ♦7 packet. Glance at the remaining 12 cards and place them at the face of the deck. Throughout the handling, remark that you are memorizing the order of the cards. By following the above procedure, the 7's are once again in their original positions in the deck.

Spread the deck face up from left to right on the table. Ask someone to point to a card. If it is just to the right of the ♣7, that card must be eleventh from the top of the deck. If the card is just to the left of the ♥7, it must be nineteenth from the top. If the card is two cards to the right of the ♠7, it must be thirty-second from the top. Thus, by noting which 7-spot the selected card is closest to, you can rapidly and silently determine its position from the top of the deck.

To perform the feat, hand out packets of cards to be shuffled. Collect them as described above. Spread the deck face up on the table.

Ask someone to point to any card. Say he selects the ♦5. Count how many cards it is from the nearest 7-spot to the selected card. Close up the spread. Pretend to perform a mental countdown. Then announce that the ♦5 is fifteenth from the top of the deck. Hold the deck face down in the left hand. Deal cards one at a time off the top into a face-up heap. When you get to the fifteenth card, it will be the ♦5. Place the dealt heap face down on top of the deck.

Repeat the feat two or three more times—the trick gains strength from repetition.

Since you know where the 7's are, you can quickly reposition them to perform the following trick, "Mind Mirror." The easiest way to do this is to place the deck behind the back, saying that you will mix the cards randomly in preparation for the next demonstration. With the deck out of sight, count to the 7's, remove them and reposition them as described below.

15. Mind Mirror

The spectator shuffles a pack of cards and divides it into three packets. He looks at a card in one packet and replaces it in the packet. The magician quickly looks over the cards in the packet, saying he is memorizing the cards. The spectator removes his card. Looking over the packet again, the magician immediately names the missing card. The trick is repeated with another chosen card.

Method: The puzzling aspect of this trick is that the spectator gives the deck a genuine shuffle. This seems to do away with the possibility of key cards, but a pair of keys is established in an offbeat way.

Place the ♣7 on top of the pack, the ♥7 twenty-sixth from the top, the ♠7 twenty-seventh from the top and the ♦7 on the bottom of the deck. The exact positions of the center cards are not critical; it only matters that they are together near the center of the deck.

Remark that you have been developing your powers of memory and would like to test your ability. As you speak, turn the deck face up so you alone can see the faces of the cards. Quickly run the cards from hand to hand until you reach the center of the deck. Split the deck between the two 7's in the center. Place the two halves of the deck face down on the table. Unknown to the audience, there is a 7 on top and bottom of both halves. Your patter line to cover this is that you want to check that there are no jokers in the deck.

Invite the spectator to riffle shuffle the two halves of the deck together. When he has given the deck one riffle shuffle, ask him to cut the deck into thirds. Indicate the bottom third of the deck. Have him remove a card from this heap, look at it, replace it on top of the heap, cut the cards and complete the cut.

Remark that you will attempt to memorize all of the cards in the heap, and that you will accomplish this by dealing through the cards only once. Hold the packet face down in the left hand. Deal cards one at a time into a heap on the table. As you deal each card, turn it face up. Watch for the red 7's. Deal the first red 7 into the face-up heap. A few more cards may have to be dealt before the second red 7 shows up. The *next* card you come to after the second red 7 will be the chosen card. Do not hesitate. Remember this card, but continue dealing all of the cards into a face-up heap.

"I think I've got them all memorized. When I turn my back, remove your card." After he has taken his card from the packet, spread the packet face up on the table. Say, "The missing card is the ♣3." Here you simply name the card you dealt after the second red 7. You will be correct.

This is an impressive feat. The audience will almost certainly ask to see it again. Point to the original top third of the deck. While you turn your back, have the spectator remove one card from this packet, look at it, place it on top of the packet, cut the packet and complete the cut.

Turn and face the audience. The handling of this packet is a little different. Place this packet face up in your left hand. State once again that you will try to memorize the cards. Deal cards off the face one at a time. Turn each card face down. Place the cards into a face-down heap on the table. Wait for the second black 7 to show up. The *next* card is the chosen card. Say this is the ♦4.

When you have finished dealing through the cards, turn your back. Ask the spectator to remove his card. Turn around, spread the cards face up on the table and announce that the missing card is the ♦4.

Choose a spectator who shuffles the cards fairly evenly. The two key cards will end up near one another after the shuffle. When the spectator later cuts the cards to lose his card in the packet, there will be little chance that he cuts between the two key cards.

16. The Memory Expert

This feat will leave no doubt in the audience's mind that you can memorize a deck of cards. Someone picks a number and remembers the card at that position in the deck. The spectator then cuts the deck and completes the cut.

You look through the deck to memorize the order. The spectator names a card, say the ♥K. Immediately you say, "The ♥K is exactly 22 cards from the top of the deck." The spectator counts off 22 cards, and the next card is indeed his card.

Now the spectator names his chosen number. Say it was 8. You say, "The card that now lies eighth from the top is the ♥A."

The spectator counts to the eighth card and it *is* the ♥A. Any borrowed deck may be used. The magician does not know the spectator's card or its original location until these facts are revealed by the spectator, yet the trick is infallible.

Method: In this simplified handling of a clever trick devised by Bob King, you need remember only two cards. Look over the faces of the cards as you pretend to check that the deck is complete. Remember the top and bottom card. We will assume the top card is the ♠A and the bottom card the ♥A. Square up the deck and place it face down on the table.

Ask the spectator to choose silently a number between 1 and 15. Have him jot it down on a piece of paper. Turn your back while this is being done. With your back still turned, ask him to count that many cards into a heap on the table.

Say he counts eight cards. Have him drop the balance of the deck on top of the dealt heap. He notes the top card of the deck, replaces this card on top, then cuts the deck and completes the cut.

Turn and face the audience. Pick up the deck. Remark that you will attempt the challenging feat of memorizing the order of all the cards in the deck. Hold the deck so you can see the faces. Beginning at the face of the deck, push cards to the right until you spot the ♠A (the original top card of the deck). Counting that card as "one," silently count all the cards to the left of it up to the top of the deck. Say you arrive at the number 22. This means that the ♠A is twenty-second from the top of the deck.

Place the deck on the table. Say, "I think I have all the cards memorized. What card did you pick?"

When the spectator names his card, pretend to think a bit, then announce, "Your card is exactly twenty-third from the top of the deck."

Deal 22 cards off the top of the deck into a heap on the table. Turn up the next card. It will be the spectator's card.

For the follow-up, replace the spectator's card face down on top of the deck. Then replace the dealt heap on top of the deck. "You gave me the name of a card and I told you its position from the top of the deck. Now let's try it the other way around. Give me the number you chose originally."

In our example the spectator chose the number 8. Pretend to think it over, then say, "If I deal eight cards from the top, the next card should be the ♥A." Here you simply name the card you originally saw on the bottom of the deck.

Deal eight cards into a heap on the table, turn up the next card and it will be the ♥A.

THE FOUR ACES

Magic with the aces has built-in appeal. Because the aces are the highest cards in the deck, it follows that if you can perform tricks with the aces, you are sure to attract the audience's attention. The tricks in this chapter feature the aces on center stage.

17. Stop at an Ace

Using any borrowed deck, the magician says he can guess which cards the spectator is probably going to pick. The magician removes the four aces. Placing the deck behind his back, the magician inserts the aces into various locations in the deck. The spectator then chooses four cards in a fair manner. They prove to be the four aces.

Method: A technique devised by Henry Christ is adapted in a clever way by Herb Zarrow to produce the four aces. When the deck is handed to you, remove the four aces. Hold the aces in the right hand, the deck in the left hand. Place both hands behind the back. When the cards are out of sight, place two of the aces face up on top of the deck. Remove two cards from the bottom of the deck. Place them face-to-face on top of the deck. Put the remaining two aces face down on top of the deck. The situation is that you have two face-down aces on top, then face-to-face indifferent cards, then two face-up aces, then the rest of the face-down deck, Figure 21.

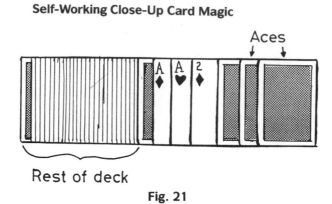

Fig. 21

Hold the face-down deck in the left hand. Explain that you want the spectator to call stop as you riffle the cards. Riffle along the left side of the deck with the left thumb, Figure 22. When the spectator calls stop, grasp the upper packet (the packet above the stop point) with the right hand as shown in Figure 23. Turn this packet over end for end onto the deck, Figure 24.

Fig. 22

Fig. 23

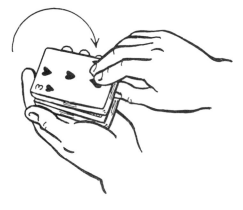

Fig. 24

Spread the cards from left to right between the hands. When you reach the first face-down card, break the deck at that point so the face-up cards are in the right hand, Figure 25. Be careful not to spread past the first face-down card.

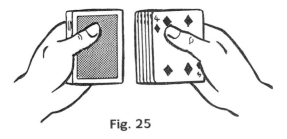

Fig. 25

The left thumb then thumbs off the top card of its packet onto the table. Turn the cards in the right hand face down and place them at the bottom of the deck.

Repeat the sequence depicted in Figures 22 through 25 in exactly the same way three more times. The result is that you will have four face-down cards on the table. Turn these cards over one at a time to reveal that you must have guessed when the spectator would call stop each time because he stopped you at the four aces.

18. Tap Reverse

The spectator picks a face-down card. When the deck is tapped against this card, a red ace mysteriously turns face up in the middle of the pack. The spectator's card is turned over. It is the matching red ace. The trick is repeated. This time the face-up card and the spectator's card turn out to be matching black aces. This routine was devised by the author.

Method: The ♠A is face down on top of the deck, followed by two face-down indifferent cards, then the face-up ♣A, then the face-down ♥A, then two face-up indifferent cards, the face-up ♦A and the balance of the face-down deck. The setup is shown in Figure 26. The group of eight cards that comprise the setup can be kept in the back pocket until you are ready to perform this trick. Have the deck shuffled. Then place it behind your back, saying that you want to hypnotize the deck so it will obey your commands. Secretly place the setup packet on top. Then bring the deck into view.

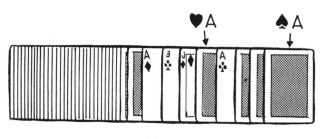

Fig. 26

Hold the deck face down in the left hand. Riffle along the left side with the thumb, as shown in Figure 22, until the spectator calls stop. Grasp the packet above the point stopped at, Figure 23, and flip it over end for end onto the deck, Figure 24.

Spread the face-up cards to the right. Stop when you get to the first face-down card. Separate the deck at that point, Figure 25. Thumb off the top card of the left-hand packet to the table.

Turn the cards in the right hand face down and replace them on top of the deck. Tap the deck against the spectator's card,

Figure 27. Then spread the cards from hand to hand. Stop when you get to the first face-up card. It will be a red ace. Cut the deck and complete the cut so the ace is on top. Then remove it and place it on the table on top of the spectator's card.

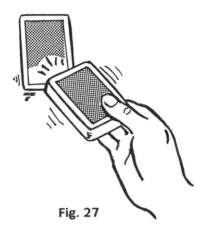

Fig. 27

Repeat the above sequence once more so that the spectator will have chosen a second card and you will have caused a black ace to turn face up. Place the black ace on top of the second chosen card.

Point to the face-up red ace. Say, "Red ace." Turn the spectator's first chosen card face up. Say, "Red ace."

Repeat with the other two cards to show another perfect match.

When riffling the cards as shown in Figure 22, be sure to begin the riffle below the setup so that the reversed cards are not exposed to the audience's view.

19. Double-Dealing

This is a routine that goes one better. Not only does the spectator find the four aces, he also finds the four kings.

Method: Beforehand place the four aces on top of the deck. The four kings are placed face up on the bottom of the deck. The setup is shown in Figure 28.

4 Aces

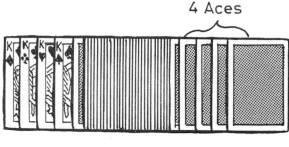

Fig. 28

When ready to perform this routine, place the pack face down on the table. Explain that you want the spectator to choose a random packet of cards in the middle of the deck. Have him cut off about half the deck, turn this portion face up and place it to the right of the other half.

Then he cuts off about half of the face-up packet and places this portion face down to the right of the other packets. The situation is shown in Figure 29.

Fig. 29

Gather the packets from left to right by placing the leftmost packet on top of the center packet, and this combined heap on top of the remaining packet.

Turn the deck over so it is face up in the hand. Fan through the face up cards until you come to the first face-down card. Cut all of the face-up cards to the bottom (or back) of the deck. Remove the group of face-down cards and give them to the spectator.

Ask him to deal out four heaps of cards. He deals one card to each heap in turn, dealing from left to right, until all of the face-down cards have been dealt.

Say, "Let's see what kind of cards you dealt yourself." Turn up the top card of each heap to reveal the four kings. Because the deck was randomly cut by the spectator, it seems no control over the cards was possible. The kings appear to show up out of nowhere.

For the double surprise finish, turn each packet over to reveal the four aces as you say, "And here's what you dealt for me."

20. Dealer's Choice

Having produced the kings and aces in the previous trick, here is a routine that uses them in a poker deal. Although the spectator dictates which cards go to which player, in the end it is seen that he gave the four aces to the magician.

Method: This trick was devised by the author. When you have finished performing "Double-Dealing" (No. 19), gather the four aces and place them face down in the left hand. Gather the four kings and place them face down on top of the aces.

Say, "First I'll mix the cards up a bit." You will perform a shuffle called an over-under shuffle. Push off the top card of the packet with the left thumb. Take it into the right hand. Push off the next card. Take it on top of the card in the right hand, Figure 30.

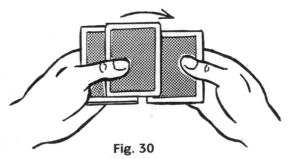

Fig. 30

Push off the next card. Take it under the packet, Figure 31. Push off the next card and take it on top of the packet. Take the next card under the packet, and so on, dealing over and under until all of the cards have been transferred to the right hand.

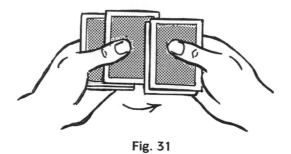

Fig. 31

Say, "And we'll give the cards a cut." Place the packet back in the left hand. Push to top two cards to the right. Transfer them to the bottom of the packet.

Deal off the top two cards. Say, "Which of these two cards do you think is an ace?" Whichever card the spectator indicates, deal it face down in front of him. Place the other card under the packet.

Deal off the top two cards. "Which of these is an ace?" Place the indicated card in front of him, the other card on the bottom of the packet.

Deal off the next pair. "Which of these is a king?" Whichever card he indicates, place that card in front of you. Put the other card under the packet. Repeat this same sequence again, giving yourself a second card.

You have four cards left. Deal off the next two cards. Ask him which he thinks is an ace. Give him that card. Put the other card under the packet.

Deal off the next pair. Whichever card he thinks is a king is placed in front of you. The other card goes under the packet.

There are two cards left. Deal the top card to him, the other card to yourself.

To conclude the trick, say with a smile, "This is a test of card sense. I'm happy that you had the good sense to give me the four aces again!" Turn up your cards to reveal the four aces.

Two of the tricks in this chapter can be routined together in the following way. Stack the ♠K face down on top of the deck, followed by the four face-down aces, the face-up ♣K, the face-down ♥K, two face-up indifferent cards, the face-up ♦K, then

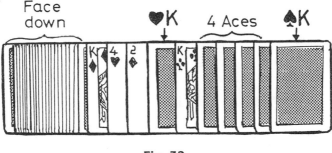

Fig. 32

the face-down balance of the deck. The setup is shown in Figure 32.

Start by performing "Tap Reverse" (No. 18). The ♥K mysteriously turns face up the first time. The ♣K will turn face up the second time. Cut the deck and complete the cut so the ♣K is on top of the deck. Deal it off. Go on to show that the kings that reversed themselves in the deck match the two kings chosen by the spectator.

Gather the four kings with one hand, the deck with the other. Place the hands behind the back. Say that you will try to guess where the spectator will cut the cards. Transfer the aces from the bottom to the top of the deck. Turn the kings face up and place them on the bottom of the deck. Bring the deck into view.

Now perform "Double-Dealing" (No. 19). If the audience wants more, you can follow with "Dealer's Choice" (No. 20).

NO-CLUE DISCOVERIES

The serious magician always has to be prepared to perform his tricks under a wide variety of close-up performing conditions. He can entertain family after dinner, or friends at parties. The tricks in this chapter were designed for special occasions when you want to baffle your audience with tricks that appear to be beyond explanation.

21. This Is Not the Card

The magician goes first. He picks a card from a shuffled deck and reverses it in position. Then the spectator picks a card and cuts it into the deck. The magician shows his card, say the ♠A. He says, "This is *not* the card you took."

The spectator agrees. The magician spells T-H-I-S I-S N-O-T T-H-E C-A-R-D Y-O-U T-O-O-K, dealing a card for each letter. "What was the card you *did* take?" The spectator might name the ♠J. The next card is turned up and it is the ♠J.

Method: What makes this trick so impressive is the seemingly random nature of the way a card is chosen. The magician never touches the card, yet it is under his direct control.

Use any shuffled 52-card deck. Ask that it be cut into three heaps, Figure 33. The heaps should be fairly even. Say, "I'm going to make a prediction, but I need a particular card."

Fig. 33

Top   Middle   Bottom

Pick up the packet on the left. Pretend to look over the faces of the cards. Really all you do is silently count the cards. Do not make it obvious that you are counting. Pause every now and then as if considering whether a particular card is the one you want. When you have counted the number of cards in the packet, replace the packet face down on the table.

Continue the count with the middle packet by picking up cards one at a time off the top, turning them face up and placing them into the left hand, Figure 34. Continue until you have counted to the twenty-ninth card. Say, "This is my prediction." Turn the twenty-ninth card face down onto the packet in the left hand. Then turn this packet over so it is face down. Replace it on the middle heap. Somewhere in this heap is your reversed prediction card.

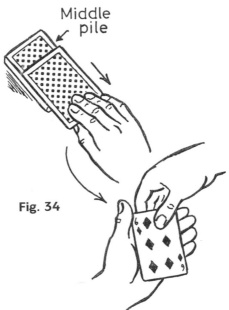

Middle pile

Fig. 34

Say, "I'd like you to take a card from the heap on the right." This is the rightmost heap in Figure 33. It has not yet been touched. Invite the spectator to shuffle this heap, note the top card and place this onto the top of the middle heap.

When he has done this, ask him to cut the middle heap and complete the cut to lose his card. Say, "I made a prediction. Let me show you which card it is." Spread through the middle heap until you get to the reversed card. Cut the packet and complete the cut so this card is on top of the heap.

"I predicted that this is not the card you took. So far I'm correct." Turn the prediction card face down on top of the middle heap. Then have the spectator place his cards (the original bottom heap) on top of the middle heap. Finally, the combined heap is placed onto the original top heap.

"Here's how the prediction works. I'm going to spell 'This is not the card you took.' We'll see how accurate the prediction really was." Spell T-H-I-S, dealing a card for each letter onto the table. Spell I-S, dealing a card for each letter. Continue in the same way for N-O-T, T-H-E, C-A-R-D, Y-O-U and T-O-O-K, dealing a card for each letter.

Say, "Now we come to the important question. What was the card you *did* take?" The spectator names his card. Turn up the top card of the deck and it will be his card.

22. Coincido

Numbers are destiny. Pick the lucky number in the lottery and your life will change overnight. Luck with numbers can be measured. In this trick, four randomly chosen numbers find a card merely thought of by a spectator. This remarkable routine was invented by Larry Jennings.

Method: Beforehand arrange to have a 10, 9, 7 and 6 on top of the deck in any order. Leave the deck in your jacket pocket until ready to perform the routine.

Get the subject of conversation around to numerology. Explain how numbers influence our lives. As you speak, place the deck on the table. Say that you would like to measure a spectator's luck with numbers. Ask the volunteer to cut the deck into four approximately equal heaps. Watch where the top portion of the deck goes. Gather the other three heaps. Ask him to give them a shuffle. Then take back this large packet of cards.

There is a small heap on the table. It is the original top portion of the deck. Turn your head aside. Ask the spectator to count the cards one at a time onto the table. He is silently to count the number of cards in the heap.

After he has done this, deal the top 20 cards of your heap in a face-up row on the table, the cards overlapping one another as shown in Figure 35. Explain to the spectator that whatever number of cards he counted, he is to look at the card in the same position in the row. For example, if he counted 12 cards in the small packet, he would look at the twelfth card, the ♣8 in Figure 35.

12th
Card

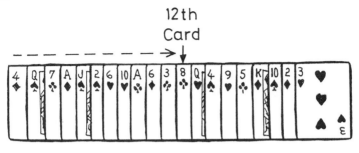

Fig. 35

Gather the spread of cards carefully so as not to disturb the order. Turn this packet face down on the table. You have a small group of cards left over in your hand. Drop this packet on top. Unknown to the audience, the spectator's card is now thirty-second from the top of your heap.

The spectator has a small packet of cards. Ask him to deal it into four piles, a card at a time, dealing from left to right until he has dealt all of the cards.

Ask him to turn up the top card of each packet. He will turn up a 10, 9, 7 and 6. He adds them together, getting a total of 32. Deal 32 cards off the top of your packet. The last card you deal is his card. Congratulate him on his luck with numbers.

23. Five-Card Mental

Allan Slaight devised a brilliant handling of a card force suggested by Dai Vernon. The spectator is handed the ♥K, ♣7, ♦A, ♥4 and ♦9, and is asked to look over the cards and merely think of one of these cards.

The magician says, "Most people would of course choose the ace because it is an obvious card. Then too, there is just one picture card in the group and that might influence your thinking. It happens there is a single black card, another obvious choice. But don't let me influence you. Silently decide on any single card."

Most people will decide on the ♥4 as the thought-of card. But if some other card is chosen, this clever method allows you to produce it in a logical manner.

Method: When you get the deck, place it below the level of the tabletop. Remark that you will try to tune in on the spectator's thought pattern. As you speak, remove the five cards mentioned above and place them on top of the deck. Reverse the ♠A and place it twelfth from the bottom of the deck.

Bring the deck into view. Ask the spectator to clear his mind of all distracting thoughts. Deal the top five cards off into a face-up row on the table in front of the spectator. As detailed above, explain why most of the cards are obvious choices. Then ask him to think of one card. After he has a card in mind, gather the cards and arrange them in the order ♥4-♣7-♥K-♠A-♦9 from the top down. Place the ♥4 off to the side face down, without showing its face, remarking that it is a troublesome card. Drop the balance of the packet on top of the deck, cut the deck and complete the cut.

Spread the cards from left to right in the hands until you reach the face-up ♠A. Cut the deck and complete the cut so the ♠A is on top of the deck. Say, "This is another troublesome card. Everyone thinks of this card." Turn the ♠A face down and place it on the bottom of the deck. Then say, "By the way, what card did you think of?"

If the spectator names the ♥4, remark, "It's a particularly troublesome card because everyone seems to think of it." Turn over the card you placed aside to show it is the ♥4.

If they name any other card, hand the deck to the spectator and have him spell out the name of his card. He deals a card for each letter, and he includes the word "of" in the spelling process. For example, if he thought of the ♣7, he would spell S-E-V-E-N O-F C-L-U-B-S, dealing a card for each letter.

If the thought-of card is black, it will show up on the final "s" of the spell. If the chosen card is red, it will show up on the card after the final "s."

24. The Square Deal

A group of 12 cards is dealt out in a 3 × 3 square by the spectator. The cards that end up in the middle of the square are turned face up and their values added together. Whatever the total, the spectator counts down to that card in the deck. The card he arrives at may be the ♦10. When a sealed prediction is opened by the spectator, it is seen that the prediction correctly foretold that the ♦10 would be chosen.

The spectator has complete freedom in the way he forms the square. Though the magician does not know ahead of time which cards will occupy any position, his prediction is always correct. The ingenious principle behind this trick was invented by Arthur Setterington.

Method: When the borrowed deck is handed to you, cut any queen to the bottom. Remove the ace through jack in mixed suits, one of each value. Begin this process by removing a jack from the deck and placing it face down on the table. Then remove a 10 and place it on top of the jack. Continue in this way up to the ace. At the conclusion you will have the 11 cards in ace-to-jack order with the ace at the top of the packet. From the audience's point of view you have simply removed a group of cards from the deck.

Run through the cards again, as if you were looking for the one card you missed. Actually, you do something quite different. Beginning at the top of the deck, silently count to the twenty-sixth card from the top. This card may be the ♦10.

Square the deck. Remove the queen from the bottom and place it on the bottom of the packet. On a piece of paper write, "You will choose the ♦10." Fold the paper and seal it in an envelope. Place the envelope in plain view.

The 12 cards are arranged in ace-to-queen order. Deal the top six cards one at a time into a heap on the table, thus reversing their order. Pick up the dealt heap and place it on top of the balance of the packet.

Hand the packet to the spectator. Invite him to cut the packet and complete the cut. He can give the packet any number of straight cuts so that he is convinced the cards are in a random order. Explain that you want him to deal the cards in a 3 × 3 square. He is first to deal three cards in a row. He can deal the row horizontally, vertically or diagonally. Say he deals the first row horizontally as shown in Figure 36.

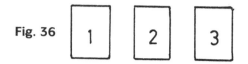

He is then to deal another row. As before, he can deal the row in any direction. The only stipulation is that it must cross the first row at the center. Say he deals this row diagonally as shown in Figure 37.

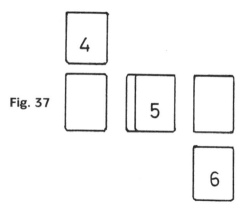

He now deals another row that crosses at the center. Say this is a vertical row, Figure 38. Finally, he deals the last three cards so as to complete the 3 × 3 square, Figure 39. You can pick up 12 cards from the top of the deck ahead of time and show him how you want him to deal the cards. Just be sure you return the 12 cards to the top of the deck after the demonstration.

Turn up the eight cards around the outside of the square. As you do, say, "Remember, you cut the packet so we wouldn't know the order of the cards. Then you dealt the cards into a square in a random order. No one could have known ahead of

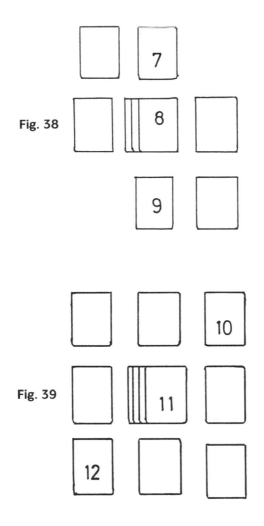

Fig. 38

Fig. 39

time which cards would be dealt where." By this time all of the cards around the border of the square have been turned face up. It is seen that they are not in any kind of order.

Hand him the face-down packet in the center of the square. It will always contain four cards. Ask him to add together the values of these cards. Jacks count 11 and queens count 12. The total will always be 26. He counts to the twenty-sixth card in the deck, and discovers that you predicted long in advance that he would choose this card.

25. A Card Is Found

Though it amounts to little more than the location of a chosen card, this routine will fool magicians as easily as it will laymen. Save it for those occasions when you want to baffle a particularly sophisticated audience. Do it once and do not repeat it, because it is a beautifully concealed swindle.

Method: This handling of an impossible-to-reconstruct card location was devised by Dai Vernon. Have a borrowed deck shuffled and cut by a spectator. Spread the deck face up on the table as you say, "That was a good shuffle. I've never seen cards so well mixed." Secretly note the value of the top and bottom cards of the deck. Suits are of no importance. Say the top card is a 7 and the bottom card an 8. Silently add the two values together. In our example you would get 15.

Gather the deck, turn it face down and hold it in the left hand. When you gather the cards, be sure not to disturb the top and bottom cards.

Begin to push cards to the right with the left thumb. Do not reverse their order. Silently count the cards until you have reached the total of the top and bottom cards. In our example you would count 15 cards. (If you can, count the cards in twos and threes. The count goes faster and it looks more random.) When you have reached a number equal to the total of the two noted cards, place this packet on the table. The top card of this packet is the original top card of the deck.

Say, "I'd like you to pick a card from the center of the deck." Start pushing cards off the top again. Say, "Just indicate where you want me to stop." Push cards into the right hand until the spectator calls stop. Place the cards in the right hand on the table to the right of the other heap.

There is a group of cards in your left hand. Say, "You stopped right here." Give the spectator the top card of the packet in the left hand. Ask him to sign his name across the face of this card.

While he does this, pick up the right-hand heap from the table and replace it on top of the cards in the left hand. Take the signed card and place it on top of these cards. Then pick up the packet that is on the table and place it on top of all. This is the original top portion of the deck.

Place the deck on the table. Say, "Finding a chosen card is like solving a mystery. The magician follows clues until he gets his man. Please cut off about two-thirds of the deck." When the spectator has done this, take the packet from him and place it face down in your left hand.

There is a small packet on the table. Turn it face up. The face card is, in this example, an 8. "That's our first clue. The card is an 8, so we count eight cards." Count eight cards off the top of your packet into a face-down heap on the table. This heap is formed to the right of the first heap.

Turn this heap face up. Point to the face card. In our example, it will be a 7. "That's our next clue, a 7. We count seven cards." Deal seven cards off the top of the packet in the left hand. Deal them into a heap on the table to the right of the other two heaps.

Turn this heap face up. Point to the face card. It might be a 10. "This is our final clue. We count ten cards." Count a fourth heap, this one containing ten cards.

"If we follow the trail to its logical conclusion, we must arrive at your card." Turn the last dealt heap face up. The face card of this heap is the card chosen and signed by the spectator.

GAMBLING TRICKS

When the gambling expert has the chance to demonstrate his skill, he always draws a crowd. This is because many of the most prized secrets are those that allow you to deal winning hands at cards. The tricks in this chapter give the reader the seemingly expert ability to control the cards in games of chance.

26. Beat the Cheat

In this impromptu poker deal, the performer first shows how a card cheat stacked the deck so he would get the aces. Then he springs a surprise. One of the honest players ends up with the aces after all. This is the author's handling of an excellent four-ace effect devised by Stewart James.

Method: Remove the four aces from a borrowed deck and place them in a face-up row on the table. Remove ten more cards from the top of the deck by pushing them into the right hand with the aid of the left thumb. As you do, remark that gamblers cheat by stacking the aces before a game of poker. Do not call attention to the number of cards taken into the right hand.

Place the deck aside for the moment. Turn one of the aces face down on the table. Deal the top three cards of the packet on top of it. Drop the balance of the packet on top of the dealt cards. Pick up the packet and place it back into the left hand. Turn a second ace face down on the table. Deal the top three cards of the packet on top of it. Drop the balance of the packet onto the dealt cards.

Continue in this way with each of the remaining aces. Say, "He stacked the aces for a four-handed game of poker." After the four aces have been stacked, hold the packet in the left hand and transfer four cards, one at a time, from the top to the bottom of the packet. As you do this, say, "One, two, three, four. That's how he stacked the deck."

Place the packet on top of the deck. Deal out four poker hands, dealing a card at a time to each player in turn until each player has five cards.

"The first player didn't have much." Turn the first hand face up, show the cards and replace the first hand on top of the deck.

"For the same reason, the third player dropped out." Turn the third hand face up, show the cards and place this hand on top of the deck.

"The second player said he suspected the dealer stacked the deck. 'I'll bet these are all aces,' he said." Turn up the middle card of the dealer's hand (the last hand) to show an ace.

"The dealer figured he could win with three aces, so he told the player to keep the ace." Turn the ace face down and slide it under the second player's hand. "The dealer took the top card of the player's hand in exchange." Remove the top card from the second player's hand and add it to the dealer's hand. It is this seemingly innocent exchange of cards that sets up the surprise finish.

"'My three aces still wins,' the dealer said." Pick up the dealer's hand. Turn the cards face up one at a time and deal them into a row on the table. The audience will be surprised to see that the dealer has *none* of the aces.

"The second player said, 'I think I can beat that hand.'" Deal out the second player's cards in a face-up row. He has the four aces, an unexpected finish to the trick.

27. Gambler's Last Chance

There was a gambler who was down on his luck, losing so often he began to wonder if he could ever win another game. During his final game, reduced to his last poker chip, he was dealt a potentially unbeatable hand. All he lacked was one card. Convinced he would lose no matter which card he was dealt, the gambler decided to let someone choose a card for him. A spectator is handed the deck. He chooses a card with the deck in his own hands. It turned out that this was *exactly* the card the gambler needed to complete a winning hand.

Method: This intriguing plot was suggested by Francis Haxton. The preparation is simple and can even be done in the course of a preliminary trick. Place the ♣9 on top of the deck and the ♠A second from the bottom. To perform the routine, spread the cards so you can see the faces. Remove the ♠10, ♠J, ♠Q and ♠K. Place them face up in a row on the table as you patter about the unlucky gambler who was dealt a potentially terrific hand.

It will be left to the spectator to pick one more card for the gambler. Spread the balance of the deck face down between the hands. Ask the spectator to remove any card. If he picks either the ♣9 or the ♠A, quit right here because he has freely chosen a card that will give the gambler a straight flush.

In the more likely case, in which the spectator takes a card from the center of the deck, have him turn his card face up. Square the deck and place the face-up card on top. Tell the spectator you are going to give him the deck behind his back. He is to insert the face-up card anywhere in the deck sight unseen. As soon as you place the deck behind the spectator's back, turn the deck over.

He takes what he thinks is the reversed card and inserts it into the center. After he has done this, ask him to cut the deck and complete the cut. He can give the deck two or three straight cuts. When he cuts the deck, his reversed card ends up between the ♣9 and ♠A. This subtle force was devised by Herb Rungie.

Reach behind the spectator's back and take the deck. Turn it over so it is face down. Bring it into view. Spread the cards face down on the table. Invite the spectator to remove the card on either side of the reversed card. If he removed the ♣9, it will give the gambler a king-high straight flush—a virtually unbeatable hand. If the spectator removes the ♠A, it will give the spectator a royal flush, the highest possible hand at draw poker. Either way, thank the spectator for his amazing ability to pick the winning card.

28. Straight Up

The magician displays a straight consisting of the ace through 5 in mixed suits, Figure 40. The cards in this poker hand are distributed to different parts of the deck, Figure 41, and slowly pushed into the deck. The magician claims he can find the straight and stack it for a two-handed game of poker, and that he can do this in less than five seconds.

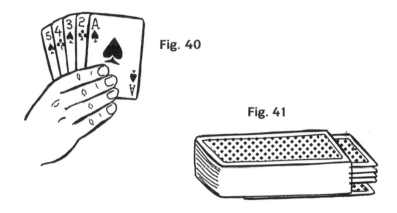

Fig. 40

Fig. 41

The magician places the deck behind his back and immediately brings it into view again. He deals two poker hands and shows that he dealt himself the straight.

Method: This clever routine was devised by Bruce Elliott. Remove the black 2's, 3's, 4's and 5's from the deck. Cut the ♠A to the face or bottom of the deck. Stack the following cards on top of the deck: X-♠2-X-♣3-X-♠4-X-♣5. (The X's indicate indifferent cards.) Place the ♣2, ♠3, ♣4 and ♠5 on the bottom of the deck and you are ready to begin.

"A gambler once published his method of stacking the deck. Only one copy of the book exists and it is kept under lock and key. A friend of mine happened to see the book and he explained the method. I'll show you." Remove the straight from the bottom of the deck. Arrange the cards in numerical order with the ♠A at the face. Display the poker hand as shown in Figure 40.

"He buried the hand in the deck." Place the ♠A on the bottom of the deck. Insert the other four cards at intervals throughout the deck, Figure 41. Slowly square the cards with the deck. "The hand has been lost in the deck. I can find it and stack the deck in less than five seconds."

Put the deck behind your back. Remove the ♠A from the bottom of the deck and place it on top. Remove the new bottom card and place it on top.

Bring the deck into view. "It's done." Deal two hands of draw poker, dealing a card to each player in turn until you each have five cards. Let the spectator look at his hand. Then turn your hand face up and show that you have dealt yourself the straight.

The trick depends on the use of card mates, that is, cards of the same value and color. When the poker hand is displayed in Figure 40, the audience sees only a tight fan of cards with the ace through 5 in numerical order. Suits are not clearly displayed. After the deal, the mates of four of these cards end up in the dealer's hand. Since the dealer gets back the most prominent card, the ♠A, the audience thinks you dealt yourself the same hand again.

29. The Lazy Gambler

"I know a gambler who's so lazy, he won't cut the cards for himself." The spectator cuts the deck. "He's so lazy, he won't stack the deck for himself. Instead, he does this." The magician gives the deck a shake. "In fact, he's so lazy, he won't even turn his own hand up to see the cards. He lets the cards do it themselves." The magician deals out two poker hands from the point where the spectator cut. The spectator gets five face-down indifferent cards. The magician's cards have mysteriously turned themselves face up. Not only that, the cards in the magician's hand are a royal flush.

Method: Stack the top ten cards of the deck as shown in Figure 42. The royal-flush cards are face down. The others are indifferent cards that are face up. They need not be the cards shown in the drawing. Just make sure they do not form a good poker hand.

When the ten cards have been stacked, gather them together without disturbing the order. Place the packet on top of

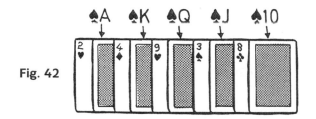

Fig. 42

the deck. As a check, the top card should be the face-down ♠10. You are now ready to perform.

As you go through the above patter line, perform the following actions. Hold the deck in the left hand. Riffle along the side of the deck with the left thumb as shown earlier in Figure 22. Do this until the spectator calls stop. The patter line is that the gambler was so lazy he would not cut the deck for himself. When the spectator calls stop, lift the packet above the point stopped at, Figure 23, and turn it over onto the balance of the deck, Figure 24.

Spread the cards from left to right until you reach the first face-down card. Take care not to spread past this point. Remove the face-up cards and place them to one side on the table.

When you say the line that the dealer was too lazy to stack the deck, shake the deck by giving the left hand a flick of the wrist. Then say that the gambler was so lazy, he would not turn his own cards face up. He let the cards turn themselves face up.

Deal out two poker hands. The spectator will get five face-down indifferent cards. You will get five face-up cards, and they will be a royal flush. This trick is an adaptation of a fine poker deal invented by Derek Dingle.

30. Test Your Skill

The advantage player knows that one card can make a difference in a poker game. The spectator is shown a group of four cards. He is asked to test his skill; can he pick out the one card that will produce an unbeatable hand? The card chosen by the spectator is reversed in the packet. The packet is dropped on top of the deck.

The performer deals out four hands of poker. The hand containing the spectator's reversed card proves to be the winner. It contains four of a kind.

Method: Arrange three groups of cards like this: A-2-3-4 A-2-3-4 A-2-3-4. Place these groups on top of the deck. Arrange another group of cards like this: 3-4-A-2. Place this group on top of the deck. Suits do not matter in this trick. Each group can have cards of mixed suits.

When you are ready to test the spectator's ability to pick the right card, remove the top four cards without disturbing their order. Ask the spectator to indicate one card. This card is turned face up and placed in position in the packet corresponding to its numerical value. The ace goes on top, the 2 second from the top, the 3 third from the top, the 4 fourth from the top. The different possibilities are shown in Figure 43. For example, if the 3 was chosen, it would be turned face-up and placed in the third position from the top as shown in *C*, Figure 43. The other cards in the packet are kept in their original order.

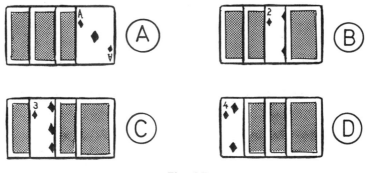

Fig. 43

Drop the packet on top of the deck. Push off the top 16 cards without disturbing their order. Ask the spectator to cut this packet and complete the cut. He then deals four poker hands, by dealing to each player in turn, a card at a time, until each player has four cards.

One hand has a face-up card in it. This is the spectator's hand. Turn up the other hands. Each of these players will have three of a kind. Turn up the hand with the reversed card. This hand contains four of a kind, beating all the other hands. Congratulate the spectator on his ability to pick the right card.

31. The Wizard of Odds

In a magic show televised in 1993, David Copperfield featured a card trick that has attracted worldwide attention. Based on a principle suggested by Jim Steinmeyer, it is the revelation of a chosen card under seemingly impossible conditions. The principle is used here for a poker demonstration. If you follow with cards in hand, you will almost certainly fool yourself with this trick.

1. Have any deck of cards shuffled and cut. Say, "The Playfair Casino sponsors a tournament in which three-card poker is played. Last week they had a million-dollar winner. I'd like to reconstruct the game with your help."

2. Take the deck. Hold it face up in the left hand. Deal nine cards into a heap on the table. As you do, remember the second card you deal. We will assume this card is the ♠A.

3. "In three-card poker, it does not matter which cards you get. The winner is the person who gets the ♠A as his hole card." Here you name the second card you dealt. Place the deck aside. Pick up the nine-card packet and turn it face down. The second card from the top of this packet is the card you glimpsed, the ♠A in our example. Hand the packet to the spectator.

4. "I'm going to turn my head aside so I can't see what you do. We're going to reconstruct that famous game. If it's done just right, we'll arrive at the same result. I'd like you to guess the dealer's name in that game. Don't tell me what name you pick. Whatever it is, I'd like you to deal one card for each letter in the name. For example, if you think the dealer's name was Joe, J-O-E has three letters, so you would deal three cards into a heap on the table."

5. Turn your head aside. Let the spectator silently choose a name. For example, if he chooses J-A-C-K, he would deal a heap of four cards. When he has done this, instruct him to drop the balance of the packet on top of the dealt heap.

6. "The casino owner was a man named James. Spell J-A-M-E-S, dealing a card for each letter into a heap." When the spectator has done this, ask him to drop the balance of the packet on top of the dealt heap.

7. "This million-dollar hand was dealt sometime between three and ten o'clock. I'd like you to guess when it happened.

Pick a number between 3 and 10. Don't tell me what number you pick. Deal that many cards into a heap on the table. In other words, if you think the winning hand was dealt at four o'clock, deal four cards into a heap."

Make it clear that the number is to be *between* 3 and 10. When the spectator has dealt the heap, ask him to place the balance of the cards on top.

8. Now have him deal three cards to the first player. Then have him deal three cards to the second player. Finally, have him deal the remaining three cards to himself. He must deal the cards one at a time into each heap, so that the order is reversed.

9. Turn and face the spectator. "Remember, the only way a player can win the big prize at three-card poker is if he has the ♠A as his hole card." As you speak, turn up the top card of each player's hand. Say, "No ♠A here, no ♠A here, no ♠A here."

10. Turn up the next card of each player's hand. Again, no ♠A shows up, Figure 44.

Fig. 44

11. "Now the tension mounts. Of course if you guessed the dealer's name correctly, and if you guessed the *exact* time the winning hand was dealt, you have nothing to worry about. Let's see who won the game."

12. Turn up the remaining card in each of the first two

hands. Then ask the spectator to turn up the remaining card in his hand. He will be amazed to learn that he has given himself the winning ♠A.

The trick can also be done over the telephone. Call a friend and ask him to remove any nine cards from the deck. Instruct him to look at and remember the top card of the packet. Then have him transfer the bottom card to the top. His card is now second from the top.

Now follow the above description of the handling, with these exceptions. In Step 4 the spectator can pick the first name of anyone in his family. In Step 6, you can use any name that spells with five letters, or an appropriate five-letter word like M-A-G-I-C. In Step 7, have the spectator choose the first name of any of his friends, as long as that name is spelled with at least three letters.

To finish the trick, ask him to take the top three cards and hold them up to the telephone. Say, "No, it's not there." Have him place the three cards aside. Repeat with the next two cards. Say, "No, not there either." Have him place those aside. Repeat with the next single card. Ask him to place that card aside.

Have him hold the next card up to the telephone. Say, "That's it!" It will always be the chosen card.

GIMMICKED CARDS

Really astounding card magic has been the specialty of many talented close-up magicians. It is not necessary to learn sleight of hand to perform many such tricks; the cards do the hard work. Gimmicked cards should be used sparingly. If the audience sees the magician do very little to accomplish a seemingly impossible feat, it will correctly conclude that the magician had help. But if a gimmicked-card trick is sprung at just the right time, it can have an enormous impact on your audience.

32. Mona Lisa

The magician reenacts the story of how the Mona Lisa was stolen by a rival of Leonardo da Vinci's. The ♥Q plays the part of the famous painting. The spectator signs his name on the face of this card. Da Vinci's rival, Leo da Quincy, substituted the ♠K. The ♠K is shown and placed against an impromptu easel. The forgery was discovered at the last minute. The ♠K is turned around to reveal that it has magically changed back to the ♥Q. The amusing presentation for this trick is from a similar effect invented by Michael Skinner.

Method: A fake card is made by cutting an index corner from a ♠K, Figure 45. On the back of the card write "FAKE!" in bold letters with a marking pen. If the writing does not stand out, place a white adhesive label on the back of the card and write "FAKE!" on the label. The writing should not extend to more than half the length of the card.

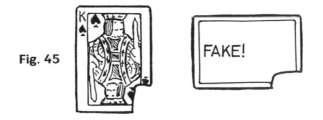

Fig. 45

The ♥Q and ♠K are placed at the face of the deck as shown in Figure 46. Cut the deck and complete the cut to bring the king and queen to the center.

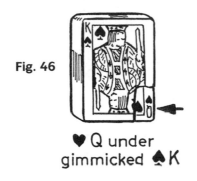

Fig. 46

♥ Q under
gimmicked ♠ K

To perform the trick, hold the cards so you can see the faces. Spread the cards from left to right between the hands. When you get to the ♥Q, cut the deck and complete the cut so the ♥Q is at the face of the deck. Lower the deck so the audience can see the ♥Q. Say, "Leonardo da Vinci's masterpiece, the *Mona Lisa*, was almost never seen by the public. We'll let this fine engraving represent the famous painting."

Deal the ♥Q to the table. Make sure the audience does not glimpse the gimmicked ♠K at the back of the deck. "Since it's difficult to write Leonardo da Vinci on a card, could you write your first name on this card?" The spectator signs the face of the ♥Q. Place the signed card on the face of the deck, cut the deck and complete the cut.

"Da Vinci's rival, Leo da Quincy, wanted to substitute a fake painting." Cut the ♠K to the face of the deck. Hold the deck with the right hand as shown in Figure 47. Turn the right hand palm down. Grasp the deck at the left end by the left hand as shown in Figure 48.

The right hand can now regrip the deck as shown in Figure 49. The fingers hide the cutout in the ♠K. The ♠K can then be displayed to the audience as indicated in Figure 49.

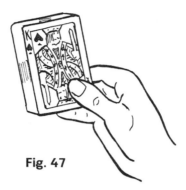

Fig. 47

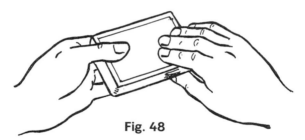

Fig. 48

Fig. 49

"Not only was he going to substitute an inferior painting, but it was a painting of a man. Worse yet, he had a *moustache!*" Turn the deck face down. Grip it by the sides with the left hand as shown in Figure 50. Here is where the gimmick comes into play. The right first and second fingers seemingly contact the face of the ♠K. But because of the cutout, they contact the face of the ♥Q and draw this card off the bottom of the deck, Figure 50. Because of the gimmick, the handling looks absolutely fair.

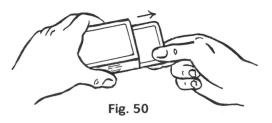

Fig. 50

Place this card against a teacup, back outward, Figure 51.

Fig. 51

"Da Vinci spotted the fake painting just before it was unveiled to the public. With a few brushstrokes he converted it back to its former glory." Blow on the card, causing it to tip over onto the table. The ♠K has magically changed back to the ♥Q.

The left hand still holds the face-down deck. The right hand cuts the top portion of the deck to the table and completes the cut. Run through the cards with the faces toward the audience. Jog the ♠K upward as in Figure 52. Close up the spread from side to side. Then lower the deck so the audience can see the writing on the back, Figure 53. "Anyone can tell the difference between a masterpiece and a fake."

To get rid of the gimmicked ♠K, turn the deck so the faces of the cards are toward you. Grip the ♠K as in Figure 47 (except that now you hold a single card rather than the complete deck).

Remove the ♠K from the deck. The back of the right hand covers the cutout. Place the ♠K in the pocket. The deck may now be used for other tricks.

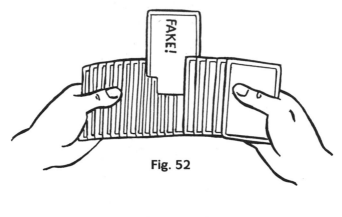

Fig. 52

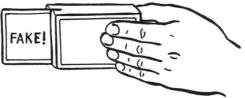

Fig. 53

33. Laser Printing

Laser printers make it possible to print instantly on practically any surface. The magician shows each of four deuces front and back. He draws a large *X* on a joker, explaining that this converts the joker into a laser printer. When the joker is placed in contact with each deuce, a large *X* magically appears on the back of the deuce. At the finish, the apparatus may be left with the audience, as there is nothing to find.

Method: Remove the four 2's from the deck. Place them face down in a row on the table. Draw an *X* on the back of each in the position shown in Figure 54, that is, near one end of the card. Place the 2's on top of the deck with the *X*'s all at the near end of the deck.

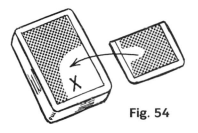

Fig. 54

Cut a joker in half. Discard one half-joker. Place the other half on top of the deck so it covers the X on the top card, Figure 54. Snap a rubber band around the deck, Figure 55. The rubber band conceals the presence of the half-card.

In your pocket have another joker and a pen.

To present the trick, hold the deck in the left hand as shown in Figure 56. Turn the hand over so the deck is face up. Withdraw the top card with the right hand as shown in Figure 57. This card is one of the deuces. Place it face up on the table.

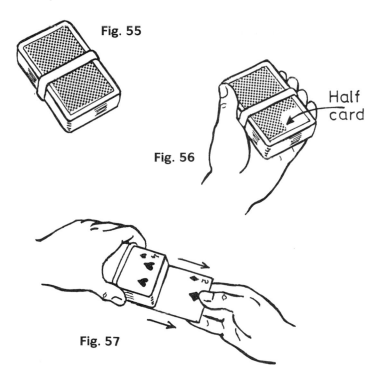

Fig. 55

Half card

Fig. 56

Fig. 57

Turn the left hand to the position shown in Figure 56 again so the audience sees the back of the top (half) card. Then turn the hand palm down and withdraw the next 2-spot as shown in Figure 57. Repeat this process with each of the other 2-spots. Because the left hand moves from the position of Figure 56 to that of Figure 57 each time, the audience thinks it sees the full back of each 2-spot. Actually, the half-card hides the *X*'s from audience view. As the 2's are removed, remark that the latest print technology is laser printing, and that you happen to have a miniature laser printer with you.

Place the deck in your jacket pocket. Remove the joker and the pen. Mark an *X* on the back of the joker near one end. Try to make the *X* resemble the *X*'s on the backs of the 2's.

Slide the joker under one of the 2's, Figure 58. Say, "Laser printing allows us to enjoy true instant printing." Turn the 2-spot face down to show that an *X* has mysteriously appeared on the back of the card.

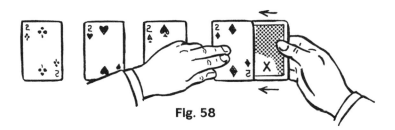

Fig. 58

Repeat with each of the remaining 2's, causing an *X* to appear on each. If you wish to perform other tricks with the deck, slide the half-card free of the deck and leave it in the pocket. Remove the deck and you are ready to perform other card tricks.

34. Simon Says

This is an ideal trick to perform at a birthday party. The birthday child and the magician each get five cards. They turn cards face up and face down to the patter of the game Simon Says. At the finish, the magician's cards are all face down. Although the child followed the magician's actions every step of the way, the child's cards are not all face down.

The trick is repeated. This time the child succeeds in matching the magician's cards and is rewarded with a special birthday prize. The child does not know why his cards did not match the magician's cards the first time, nor does she know why they did match the second time. It is a puzzling feat with a happy ending.

Method: This handling of a classic effect is based on ideas of Clayton Rawson and the author. The trick uses what, in magician's parlance, is known as a double-backed card.

Put some glue or rubber cement on the face of a card. Then place another card on top of it so the two cards are face to face, Figure 59. Make sure the cards are perfectly aligned. When the glue has dried, you will have a double-backed card, that is, a card that shows a back on each side. Place the double-backed card ninth from the top of the deck and you are ready to perform.

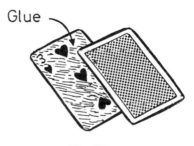

Glue

Fig. 59

At a birthday party or other special event, invite the guest of honor to participate. Say, "Do you know how to count to 5?" Have the child count aloud as you deal five cards into her hand from the top of the deck.

"Can you count to 5 again?" Deal five more cards off the top of the deck. Place the deck aside. Pick up the second group of five cards and place it in your left hand. Unknown to the audience, you have a double-backed card second from the top of your packet.

"Do you know the game of Simon Says? You have to do what I do, but only if I says 'Simon says.'" You and the child then perform the following actions with your respective packets of cards:

1. "Simon says to turn the top card face up and place it on the bottom."

2. "Simon says to put the next card face down on the bottom."

3. "Simon says to turn the next card face up and put it on the bottom."

4. "Simon says to put the next card on the bottom."

When this series of actions has been performed, say, "Let's see if everything is the same." Spread your cards to show that every other card is face up. The child spreads her cards and shows that every other card is also face up. "Great. We match. Now comes the hard part." You and the child now perform these actions with your respective cards.

5. "Simon says to turn the entire packet over."

6. "Simon says to turn the top card face down."

7. "Simon says to turn the entire packet over."

8. "Simon says to turn the top card face up."

9. "Simon says to turn the entire packet over."

Spread your cards. All the cards are face down. The child spreads her cards. One card is face up. "Gee, you almost got it. Let's try it again. This time, for good luck, we'll use your name." If the child's name is Dina, each time you will use the phrase "Dina says" instead of "Simon says." Start with all cards face down. Make sure the double-backed card in your packet is second from the top. Repeat Steps 1 through 4. Stop and check that the child's cards match yours.

Now repeat Steps 5 through 8. Do *not* perform Step 9. The child spreads her cards and finds one reversed in the middle. "If your cards match mine, you win the prize." Spread your cards face up to show one card reversed in the middle. "You did it!" Congratulate the child and hand her the prize.

35. Chase the Ace

"Chase the Ace" is one of the best of all small-packet tricks. The magician shows two black kings and a red ace, Figure 60. The ace is unmistakably in the center between the kings. The packet is closed up and turned over. The magician says, "Where's the ace now?" The spectator thinks the performer did some kind of sleight of hand.

"I'll give you a hint." The magician fans the packet. The spectator is surprised to discover that the center card has somehow reversed itself and is now face down, Figure 61.

"It should be obvious. Where's the ace?" The spectator points to the center card. When the magician turns this card over, it has changed to the ♣J, Figure 62. The elusive ace is then removed from the card case!

"Chase the Ace" can be carried in the pocket. The magic is visual and startling, and the trick is always ready to work.

Fig. 60

Fig. 61

Fig. 62

Method: A single gimmicked card is responsible for all of the changes. Cut the index corner from an ♦A. The dimensions shown in Figure 63 are for a poker-size card. If you use bridge-size cards, the width of the gimmick should be about ⅛″ rather than ¼″.

Glue the gimmick to the back of a ♣J, Figure 64. Place a ♣K face up on the table, then the face-down ♣J, then a face-up ♠K. Finally, place the three cards plus an ungimmicked ♦A in the card case. This completes the preparation.

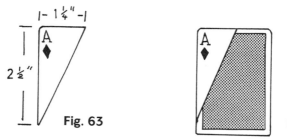

Fig. 63   Fig. 64

When ready to perform, leave the ♦A in the card case and take out the other three cards. Say, "I played a game of three-card monte the other day. Here's what happened." Fan the three cards and hold them in the right hand as shown in Figure 65. Be sure to fan the cards with the proper end of the gimmicked card uppermost. The fingers hide the bottom of the gimmicked card.

Show the faces of the cards. The audience sees the cards as depicted in Figure 65. "The gambler used two black kings and a red ace. The ace was definitely in the middle."

Fig. 65

Place the left palm against the faces of the cards. Use the left fingers to square the packet. Lower the left hand so the backs of the cards can be seen by the spectators, Figure 66.

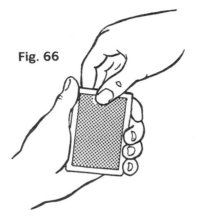

Fig. 66

Grasp the front of the packet with the right hand, thumb on top, fingers below, as depicted in Figure 66. Turn the packet end for end into the left hand. Do this twice more. The packet will be face up. "He turned the cards over and over like this. I knew he was using sleight of hand. He said, 'Where's the ace now?'"

The audience might say the ace is still in the middle, or it might voice suspicion. Whatever it says, you reply, "Of course I was suspicious. This fellow gave me a big hint." Fan the cards between the hands, Figure 67. This is the first surprise; the center card has turned face down.

Fig. 67

"Where's the ace? I thought it was obvious. But when I turned over the middle card, I got a surprise." Grasp the center card as shown in Figure 68. Turn it over, Figure 69, and toss it to the table. This is done with one quick gesture. The audience does not have a change to glimpse the ♦A index on the back of this card. They see that the middle card has changed to a jack.

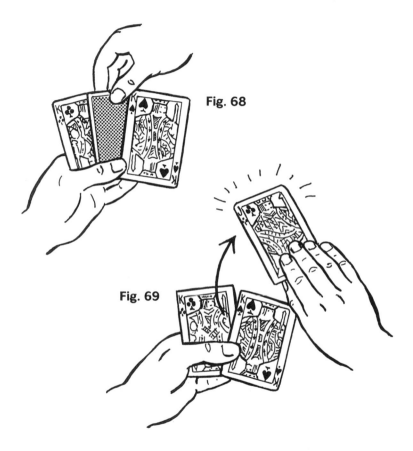

Fig. 68

Fig. 69

"That's when I learned never to bet on the other man's game." Drop the kings one at a time onto the table. "When it came to finding the ace, I was looking in the wrong place." Slowly remove the ♦A from the card case.

When you turn over the packet as depicted in Figure 66, you can end this maneuver with a magical-looking flourish. Place the packet face down in the left hand. Grasp the front of the packet as shown in Figure 66 and turn the packet over end for end. The packet is now face up. Repeat the turnover a second time to bring the packet face down. For the final turnover, hold the packet in the left hand as shown in Figure 66, then turn the hand palm down and push the packet through the hand as shown in Figure 70. Go on from there to spread the packet as shown in Figure 67, and finish the routine as written.

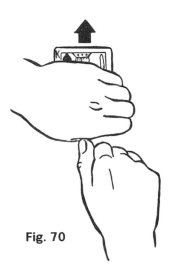

Fig. 70

36. McDonald's Aces

Mac McDonald invented an ace assembly that has become a magic classic. Three aces vanish one at a time, only to reappear with the ♠A. As closely as the audience watches, it cannot see how the aces vanish. The reappearance of the aces comes as a genuine surprise.

Method: Three double-face cards are used. Glue the ♣5 back to back with the ♣A, the ♥3 back to back with the ♥A, and the ♦2 back to back with the ♦A. Place these three cards on the bottom of the deck with the ♣5, ♥3 and ♦2 facing outward. Then place an ordinary card on the bottom of the deck. If the deck is turned face up, the stack at the face of the deck would look as shown in Figure 71.

A duplicate ♣A, ♦A and ♥A are added to the deck. These three aces plus the ♠A are distributed in the top two-thirds of the deck.

When you are ready to perform this routine, spread the deck face up on the table. Remove the four ordinary aces. Keep the ♠A apart from the other three aces. The situation is shown in Figure 71.

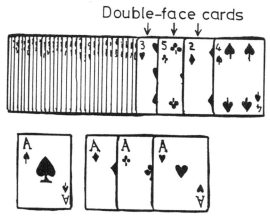

Fig. 71

Remark that a gambler named McDonald once figured out a way to attract good cards to his own poker hand. As you speak, square up the ♦A, ♣A and ♥A. Keep them in that order, with the ♥A at the face.

"We'll use some other cards for the poker hands." Square the deck, but leave it face up. Lift off about half the cards from the face of the deck. Turn this packet face down and drop it on top of the face-up packet of three aces. Put the rest of the deck aside.

Push off four cards and place them to the left on the table. Push off another four cards and place them to the right of the first four-card group. Push off four more cards and place them to the right of the other groups. As you do this, say, "It was a four-handed game." Indicate that the ♠A will be the basis for the fourth hand.

You still have a group of cards in your left hand. Push cards over until you get to the first face-up ace. This is actually a double-face card, but to the audience it appears to be the original ♦A. The face-down cards above the double-face cards are placed aside and are not used.

Deal the ♥A on the left heap, the ♣A on the middle heap and the ♦A on the right heap. These are the three double-face cards. You will be left with a group of four cards. Keep these cards carefully squared. Drop this packet on top of the ♠A. The layout looks as shown in Figure 72.

Fig. 72

"The first fellow had the ♥A. McDonald thought this would be a good card for his hand." As you speak, pick up the left-hand packet and place it in the left hand. Transfer the ♥A to the back or bottom of the packet. Push over the top card of the packet and transfer it to the bottom of the packet. Turn the packet over end for end three times and replace it in the left hand. (All of the handling described in this paragraph is a bit of hocus-pocus to misdirect the audience's attention; you do not want it to know the exact location of the ace.)

"When McDonald snapped his fingers, the ace disappeared." Turn the left hand palm down and thumb off the bottom card, Figure 73. Turn the hand palm up. Thumb off the next card (the double-facer), Figure 74. Turn the hand palm down. Deal the next card face down to the table. Turn the hand palm up. Thumb off the next card to the table. Turn the hand palm down and toss the last card face down to the table. The hand thus turns palm

Fig. 73

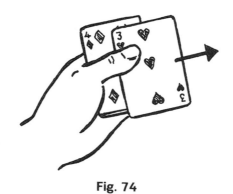

Fig. 74

down, palm up, palm down and so on, so that face-up and face-down cards alternate on the table. When doing this, try to keep the hand turned inward toward the body so the audience does not get a clear glimpse of the identity of any of the face-down cards.

There are three face-down cards on the table. Turn them face up one at a time to reveal that the ♥A has vanished.

Repeat the above sequence with the ♣A packet, and then with the ♦A packet. Take your time turning up each of the face-down cards. The vanish of the aces is deceptive and visually very strong.

"McDonald figured he had a pretty good hand by this time." Spread the cards in the ♠A packet to show the four face-up aces. These are ordinary cards and may be used in other tricks.

THE THREE-JACKS DEAL

This very clever deal has about it the aura of great skill. As you deal two poker hands of three cards each, you show that the player's hand has three jacks. The deal is repeated and once again the player gets three jacks. The effect may be repeated indefinitely. Over the years a number of refinements have been made to this trick. They are described here so the reader has access to the latest thinking on this classic effect.

37. Jack Jack Jack

The effect is one in which the magician always deals three jacks to the same hand, no matter how many times he deals the cards. No skill is required, and the trick resets automatically.

Method: Arrange four jacks as follows from the top down: J-J-J-*X*-J, then the rest of the deck. The letter "*X*" represents any card.

Deal two hands of three cards each. Do this by dealing the first card to the player, the second card to the dealer, the next card to the player and so on, alternating a card to each person until each has three cards.

As you are about to deal the third card to the dealer, an important part of the handling takes place. You will use the third card to scoop up the dealer's hand and replace it on top of the deck. The details are as follows. Place the left fingertips against the first two cards in front of the dealer, Figure 75. This is done to steady these two cards and keep them in place. The right hand holds the dealer's third card. Use this card as a scoop; slide it under the dealer's first two cards, Figure 76, and place this three-card hand back on top of the deck. You do not need to hold the deck when doing this move. You can put the deck down so the left hand is free to aid in the scooping action. This handling must be done on each deal for this trick and all other tricks in this chapter in order for the trick to work.

Player's hand

Fig. 75

Dealer's hand

Fig. 76

Turn up the player's hand. It will contain three jacks. Your patter is about a gambler who had the uncanny ability to deal himself three jacks when he wanted. As you show the player's hand, say, "Let me show you again."

Drop the three jacks on top of the deck. With no adjust-
ments, you can repeat the deal. Deal three cards to each player
as before. Remember to use the dealer's third card to scoop up
the other two cards as shown in Figure 76. The dealer's hand is
never shown. After it is scooped up, it is dropped on top of the
deck. All attention is on the player's hand. No matter how often
you repeat the deal, the player will get three jacks.

38. Three-Jacks Improved

The key to the Three-Jacks Deal is that you are really dealing
three out of four jacks to the player each time. The result is that
sometimes he will have two red jacks and one black jack, and
sometimes he will have two black jacks and one red. Most people will not notice the discrepancy, but if you are working for fast
company, Walter Gibson devised a clever way to produce two
red jacks and one black jack every time.

The setup is as follows: red jack–black jack–red jack–*X*–black
jack, then the rest of the deck. The setup is the same as the original except that the colors of the jacks alternate.

Deal two hands of three cards each. Scoop up the dealer's
hand as shown in Figure 76 and replace it on top of the deck.
Turn up the player's hand to show three jacks.

The key ingredient comes into play at this point. Take the
facemost jack (a red jack) and use it to scoop up the other two
jacks, Figure 77. This puts the black jack in the center between
two red jacks. Turn the jacks face down and put them on top of
the deck.

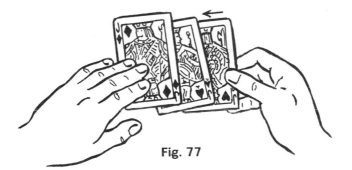

Fig. 77

Repeat the deal exactly as described above. The player will get three jacks again, two reds and a black. The black jack will change from the ♠J to the ♣J, but this is a small point that will almost never be noticed. When spreading the player's hand, spread it just enough so he sees three jacks, but not so much that he has a chance to study the suits.

The deal may be repeated four or five more times.

39. Unstacked Jacks

Jack Potter suggested an opening trick for the Three-Jacks Deal that produces a startling effect. Using a borrowed, shuffled deck, the magician openly removes the three jacks and places them on the table. "Some gamblers stack the deck ahead of time. This is how they do it." The magician places the top card of the deck on the table. Then he places a jack on top of this card. He takes another card from the top of the deck and places it on the jack. Then he places a second jack on top of this card. A third card is taken from the top of the deck and placed on top of the heap. Then the third jack is placed on top of the heap.

The heap of six cards is placed on top of the deck. "Now the gambler is ready. When he deals a two-handed game, he will get the jacks. However, I don't have to set up the cards ahead of time."

The magician deals the top three cards into a face-up heap. They are the three jacks!

Method: When you are handed the deck, look through the cards until you spot a black jack. Cut the deck and complete the cut so this jack is third from the top at the completion of the cut.

Run through the cards and remove the other three jacks. Place them face down on the table. You will have two red jacks and one black. Make sure the black jack is the top card of the jack packet.

Patter about the way gamblers stack the deck before a game. Place the top card of the deck on the table. Show the face of the black jack and put it on top of this card. Place the new top card of the deck on top of the black jack. Show the face of a red jack and place it on the heap. Take the top card of the deck and put it on the heap. Show the face of the other red jack and put it on top of the heap. Then drop the six-card heap on top of the deck.

"That's how some gamblers stack the deck ahead of time. I don't have to do that." The audience just saw you alternate three jacks with three other cards. When you deal the top three cards face up onto the table and they are three jacks, it is a surprising sight.

"Experts can stack the cards instantly." Cut the jack packet and complete the cut so the black jack is between the two red jacks. Drop the jack packet on top of the deck. Now perform "Jack Jack Jack" (No. 37) exactly as described and the player will get three jacks.

40. Three Jacks and a Pat

In its classic form, the Three-Jacks Deal lacks a finish. Phil Weisbecker invented a version where you end with the dealer getting a royal flush.

Method: From the top down, the stack is as follows: ♠J-♣J-♥J-♠A-♦J-♠K-any ace-♠Q-ace-♠10, then the rest of the deck.

To perform the trick, explain that you have been taking a course on how to spot card cheats. One lesson explained how gamblers slip three jacks into the player's hand. Deal two hands of three cards each. Scoop up the dealer's hand as shown in Figure 76 and replace it on top of the deck. Turn up the player's hand to show three jacks.

Cut the odd-color jack to the center of the player's hand. Drop the hand on top of the deck. "Let me show you again." Repeat the deal. Show that the player got three jacks. Cut the odd-color jack to the center of the player's hand and replace the hand on top of the deck.

"If you don't know what to look for, it's not easy to spot the move." Repeat the deal one more time. Show that the player got three jacks. Cut the ♠J to the center of the player's hand. Drop the hand on top of the deck.

"Last week we learned how to spot the move in a regulation game." Deal two hands of five cards each. Turn up your opponent's hand. "Three jacks and two aces for a full house. If you want to beat a strong hand like that, here's a valuable tip: Deal yourself an even better hand."

Deal your cards into a face-up row on the table in ace-to-10 order, revealing that you dealt yourself a royal flush.

41. Progressive Poker

Walter Gibson popularized a repeat poker deal that has become a magic classic. In the original routine the gambler showed he could deal himself three jacks whenever he wanted. When a neophyte tried it, he failed. The trick was repeated, with a surprise finish.

This is the author's adaptation of the Gibson routine. The trick begins with the gambler dealing several three-card hands. Each time he gets three jacks. Then he deals four-card hands and still gets three jacks. Finally he deals five-card hands and still gets three jacks. When the neophyte tries it, he deals himself a full house. He thinks he has won, but the gambler has a royal flush.

Method: A ten-card set-up does all the work. From the top down, the stack is ♣J-J-J-♣Q-J-♣A-♣10-9-♣K-9, then the balance of the deck.

"A gambler who won a fortune at poker said that through years of practice, he could deal himself three jacks any time he wanted to."

As you talk, deal out two hands of three cards each. Deal a card to the player, a card to yourself, a card to the player and so on, until each of you has three cards. Use your last card to scoop up the other two cards in your hand, as shown in Figure 76. (You will repeat this handling of the dealer's cards on each round.) Put your hand on top of the deck. Turn up the player's cards and fan them to show three jacks. Drop the hand face down on top of the deck.

"It works every time." Deal two more hands of three cards each. Again show that the player was dealt three jacks.

"A beginner sitting at the table said, 'Can you do it with hands of four cards each?' The gambler said, 'Sure.'"

Deal two hands of four cards each. Show that once again the player was dealt three jacks. Handle them as before, first scooping up the dealer's hand and placing it on top of the deck, then placing the player's hand on top of the deck.

The beginner said, "That looks easy. Let me try it." Playing the part of the beginner, deal two hands of four cards each. Turn up the player's hand. "But the beginner got only two jacks." After you show that the player didn't get three jacks, drop the hand on top of the deck.

"The gambler said, 'It's all in the way you slip yourself that extra jack.'" Deal two more hands of four cards each. Show that the player once again got three jacks.

"The beginner said, 'In regulation poker, each player gets five cards.' The gambler nodded. 'Works with five cards too.'" Deal two hands of five cards each. Show that the player got three jacks.

"The beginner said, 'I saw you slip that card. Let me try it.'" Deal two hands of five cards each. Turn up the player's hand to show that he dealt himself only two jacks.

"The beginner couldn't understand what went wrong. The gambler said, 'I'll show you why it doesn't work when you do it. Deal another round.'" Deal out two hands of five cards each. Scoop up the dealer's hand as in Figure 76, turn it face up and fan the cards. "The gambler said, 'You've been dealing *me* the three jacks.'" Show that the dealer's hand has three jacks. Turn this hand face down and drop it on top of the deck. Then drop the player's hand on top of the deck.

Give the deck to the spectator. "Now the beginner knew how to do it." Ask the spectator to deal out two hands of five cards each. Turn up his hand. "Not only did he get three jacks, he got a pair of 9's. The beginner smiled triumphantly and said, 'There you are, an unbeatable full house.'"

Deal the gambler's hand face up, a card at a time. "The gambler said, 'A full house, yes. Unbeatable, no.'" Show that you have a royal flush.

The hands can be summarized as follows:
1. Three cards to each hand. Player gets three jacks.
2. Same as 1.
3. Four cards to each hand. Player gets three jacks.
4. Four cards to each hand. Players gets a pair of jacks.
5. Four cards to each hand. Player gets three jacks.
6. Five cards to each hand. Player get three jacks.
7. Five cards to each hand. Player get two jacks.
8. Five cards to each hand. Dealer gets three jacks.
9. Spectator deals five cards to each hand. He gets full house. Magician gets royal flush.

The setup can be written on the inside of the flap of the card case for easy reference. You deal two rounds of three cards each, three rounds of four cards each, and four rounds of five cards each. The increasing number of cards makes it seem that much more skill is called for, but the setup produces the right cards on every round.

NOVELTY CARD TRICKS

The novelty card trick has traditionally been used as a change of pace between more serious mysteries. "Once you have practiced magic for a while," J. W. Sarles wrote, "you develop an appreciation for unusual or offbeat effects." A trick built around a novel premise will amuse and entertain, even as it baffles the audience.

42. Spell Purple

Many spelling tricks with cards require an elaborate setup. This routine, devised by gambling expert John Scarne and the author, is impromptu and has the unique feature that the spectator sets up the cards for you.

The trick is one where the magician spells "R-E-D," transferring a card at a time from the top to the bottom of a packet for each letter. When he turns up the next card, it is a red card. He spells "B-L-A-C-K" and turns up a black card. The trick proceeds to a surprise conclusion.

Method: Before doing the trick, slip a pen into your jacket sleeve or back pocket. If you wear a watch, slide it under the band so it will stay in place. When you are seated opposite the spectator, ask him to remove two clubs from the deck and place them face down on the table. Then have him remove two diamonds and place them on top of the clubs. Next he removes two spades and places them on top of the diamonds. Finally, he removes two hearts and places them on top of the spades.

Take the packet from him. Remark that you are going to program the cards for a spelling bee. Lower the packet out of sight below the level of the tabletop. Quickly deal the cards from hand to hand, reversing their order. The clubs are now on top, followed by the diamonds, spades and hearts in that order.

If the spectator's name has either three or six letters, write his name on the face (or bottom) card of the packet. Examples of three-letter names might be Bob, Jim or Eve. Examples of six-letter names might be George, Sandra or Robert. If your friend does not have a name that fits either of these categories, write "PURPLE" on the face card. Then hide the pen back in the sleeve.

Bring the packet into view. "This is a remarkable program that produces cards just by spelling to them." Spell "R-E-D," dealing a card from the top to the bottom of the packet for each letter. When you have completed the spelling, say, "I spell red and we get a red card." Turn up the top card of the packet. It will be a red card. Place it on the table.

Spell "B-L-A-C-K," dealing a card from the top to the bottom of the packet for each letter. "I spell black and get a black card." Turn up the top card. It is black. Place it on the table.

Use the same procedure to spell "R-E-D," producing another red card. Place the red card on the table. Then spell "D-I-A-M-O-N-D" using the same spell-count procedure. Turn up a diamond and place it on the table. Follow the spell-count procedure for "S-P-A-D-E." Turn up a spade and put it on the table.

"It even works for other colors, for example, purple." Spell "P-U-R-P-L-E," dealing a card from top to bottom for each letter. "We spell purple and get purple." Pause for dramatic effect. The audience will watch closely, knowing there are no purple cards in the deck. Turn up the top card. It has "PURPLE" written on it.

If you plan to perform this trick at a party, beforehand remove the ♥4 from the deck. Color over the pips with a purple marking pen. Conceal the purple ♥4 in the jacket sleeve. When the packet of eight cards is handed to you, hold it below the level of the tabletop, and arrange it in clubs-diamonds-spades-hearts order as described earlier. Remove the bottom card of the packet (a heart) and put the purple ♥4 in its place. The ordinary heart may be concealed in the jacket sleeve or on the lap.

Perform the routine as described above. At the finish you will produce a card that is indeed purple.

If you wish to personalize the trick by using the spectator's name, proceed as follows. As described above, you would take the packet behind your back, or under the table, reverse the order of the cards and write your friend's name on the bottom card of the packet. Say the name is Sandra.

Proceed with the trick as described, up through the point where you spell "S-P-A-D-E" and turn up a spade. Then say, "It works for names too. For example, your name is Sandra. We spell 'S-A-N-D-R-A.'" Do this, transferring a card from top to bottom for each letter. "And we get a Sandra." Turn up the next card to reveal a card with "Sandra" written on the face. This only works for names which contain three, six or nine letters (in other words, any multiple of three). The spectator you do it for should be delighted that his or her name figured so prominently in a card trick.

43. Pushbutton Magic

After a spectator makes a selection with the cards in his own hands, the magician remarks that pocket calculators now have the capability to reveal which card was chosen. The magician enters a series of numbers into a pocket calculator, does some quick math and comes up with the number 49, as shown in Figure 78. "You didn't pick the 49 of clubs, did you?" the magician asks. The spectator answers no.

"49 is 7 squared. It wasn't the 7 of diamonds, was it?" The spectator answers no.

The magician snaps his fingers. "Of course. The prediction was upside down." He turns the calculator around. It shows a

Fig. 78

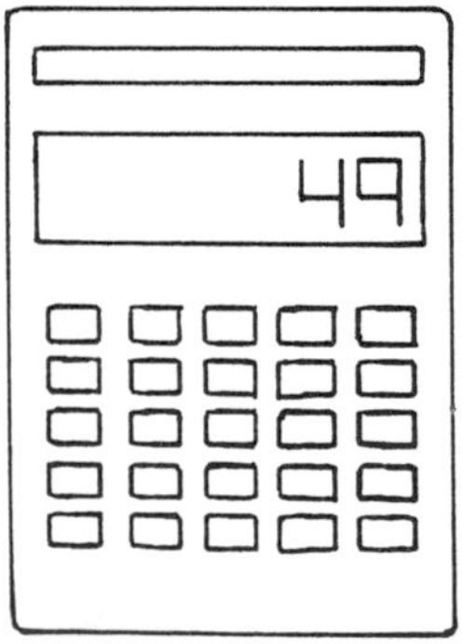

"6" and an "h," indicating the ♥6, Figure 79. "Did you pick the
♥6?" In fact, that is exactly the card chosen by the spectator.

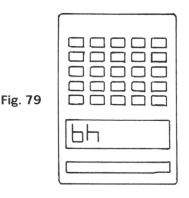

Fig. 79

Method: Without letting the audience see the faces of the
cards, remove four hearts from the deck. They can be any values
above 6, for example, the ♥8, ♥10, ♥J and ♥Q. Put these four
cards in a face-down heap on the table in front of you. Then
remove the four 6's and place them face down on top of the
heap. The rest of the deck is placed aside. As you remove the
cards, say, "Even magic is getting automated. Now they have
card tricks in which a pocket calculator figures out what card
you chose."

Hand the packet of eight cards to the spectator. Ask him to
cut the packet and complete the cut. He can do this any number
of times until he is satisfied the cards are in a random order.

Explain that you want him to transfer the top card to the
bottom of the packet. He is then to deal the next card to the
table. The next card is transferred to the bottom of the packet.
The next card is dealt to the table. He continues this duck-and-
deal procedure until he has two cards left.

Say to him, "One card has a lower value than the other. Use
the value of that card. Use the suit of the other card. By this
method we arrive at a random card that the calculator couldn't
possibly know."(By means of the duck and deal, the spectator
will always be left with a 6 and a ♥.)

"Don't show me your cards. I want the calculator to figure
this out." Use any pocket calculator. Start pressing buttons. Half
to yourself, say, "We take the population of the United States,
divide it by the rainfall in Peru, multiply by the number of cars

sold in Canada last year, and that tells me——" Stop as if you just realized something is wrong. "That tells me I forgot to turn on the calculator."

Turn on the calculator. Holding it so no one else can see the buttons, rapidly press the plus, minus and multiply buttons as if you were making quick calculations. Then enter a 4 and a 9. Turn the calculator so the audience sees the face. It will look like Figure 78.

"By any remote chance, did you pick up the ♣49?" The spectator will answer no. "49 is 7 squared. Was it the 7 of diamonds?" Once again the spectator will answer no.

"Let's see your two cards." One will be a 6 and the other a ♥. "This indicates you picked the ♥6." Act puzzled, then snap your fingers. Turn the calculator around so it looks like Figure 79. The calculator knew the spectator would pick the ♥6.

44. Tale of the Tape

George Blake has pioneered tricks using tape recorders. In this routine, a taped message instructs the spectator how to choose a card from the deck. The card is buried in the deck. Then the taped message finds the card and reveals its identity.

Once you record the instructions, the cassette tape can be carried with you. Slip it into any cassette recorder, press the play button, sit back and let the tape perform an offbeat mystery.

Method: Before performing the trick, cut the ♠A to the top of the deck. The rest of this description consists of the message recorded on the cassette tape.

"Deal two equal heaps of cards on the table by dealing a card to your left, one to your right, one to your left, and so on. It doesn't matter how many cards you deal. Just make sure the two heaps are equal."

(After the audience hears this instruction, push the pause button, stopping the tape until the spectator has dealt the two heaps. Then push the play button.)

"Good. Transfer the bottom card of the left-hand packet to the top of that packet. Make some kind of mark on the back of the top card. Don't show me what mark you chose."

(Stop the tape until the spectator has done this. Then push the play button.)

"Take a little more than half the cards from the right-hand packet. Put them on top of the left-hand packet. Pick up the left-hand packet. Place the top card of this packet on top of the deck. Put the bottom card on top of the deck. Put the top card on top of the deck, then the bottom card, and so on until all cards have been dealt onto the deck."

(Make sure the spectator takes top and bottom cards alternately until he has dealt all of the cards onto the deck.)

"Take *one* card from the right-hand packet and place it on the bottom of the deck. Then deal the remainder of the right-hand packet into a row on the table.

"Put the deck into your left hand. Deal one card off the top of the deck onto each of the cards on the table."

(After this instruction has been given, stop the tape until the spectator has completed this step.)

"It looks to me as if your card is on top of the deck. I'd recognize that mark anywhere. Hold the marked card close to the tape recorder. Closer. Good. I can see it clearly. It's the ♠A. Thank you!"

45. A Word in Thousands

The spectator calls out a number, say 11. He counts down to the eleventh card in the deck, which we will say is a 5-spot. He picks up the book you are now reading, takes it to a corner of the room, opens it to the beginning of any chapter, and notes the fifth word in the opening sentence.

The magician, standing some distance away with his back turned, immediately reveals the chosen word.

Method: The book you are now reading, *Self-Working Close-Up Card Magic*, has been set up as a force book. Open the book to the first page of any chapter. The fifth word in the opening sentence will be "has." This is true even if the spectator opens the book to the Introduction.

It is necessary to force a 5-spot. A subtle method is as follows. Before performing this trick, arrange to have any 5-spot fourth from the top of the deck.

Write "has" in large letters on a sheet of paper, fold the paper and place it in full view.

Ask the spectator to name a number between 10 and 30.

Whatever number he names, silently add 3 to it. For example, he names 11. Add 3, arriving at 14.

Count 14 cards off the top of the deck one at a time into a heap on the table. Then pretend to realize you made a mistake. "Wait. You didn't say 14. You said——." Hesitate and look at the spectator. He will say 11.

Say, "Right. Maybe you had better count the cards." Put the 14-card heap back on top of the deck. Give him the deck. Ask him to count to the eleventh card. It will be the 5-spot.

Tell him to take the book to a far corner of the room, open it to the beginning of any chapter and note the word at the position corresponding to the value of the card. Say, "For example, if you picked a 3, you would look at the third word. If you picked a 4, you would look at the fourth word, and so on."

Have him name his chosen word. Then show that you were correct.

46. Tic-Tac-Toe

This is a unique game of tic-tac-toe. The spectator shuffles the deck and cuts it into two heaps. He shuffles one heap and keeps it for himself. Then he shuffles the other heap and gives it to the magician.

The players take turns drawing cards from their respective packets. If the first player draws, say, a 7, he places an O in the space labeled "7" in Figure 80. If the other player draws a "3," he places an X in the space labeled "3."

The game continues until one player has three O's or three X's in a row. That player is the winner. The magician will always win.

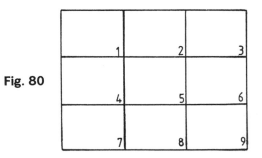

Fig. 80

Method: Remove from the deck all the even-value cards 2, 4, 6, 8 and place them in one heap. Remove all the odd-value cards A, 3, 5, 7, 9 and place them in a separate heap. Transfer two 4's from the even heap to the odd heap. Transfer two 3's from the odd heap to the even heap.

Place the even heap face down in front of you. Place the 10's through kings on top. Place the odd heap on top of all. Then deal the deck into two heaps by dealing a card to the left, one to the right, one to the left, one to the right, and so on, until the entire deck has been dealt into two heaps.

Draw the layout like the one shown in Figure 80 on a piece of paper that measures slightly smaller than a playing card. Place the paper on top of one heap. Put the other heap on top of all. Case the deck until the time of performance.

The idea behind the above stack is that if you have all the odd-value cards, you cannot lose. By giving the spectator a couple of 3's, and yourself a couple of 4's, you disguise the setup.

When ready to perform the trick, remove the deck from the case. Explain that you want to play a game of tic-tac-toe in which the moves are left completely to chance. Cut the deck at the layout. Place the two halves alongside one another. Push the layout toward the spectator. If he can give the cards an even riffle shuffle, let him riffle shuffle the two halves together. If he cannot, perform the shuffle yourself.

After the shuffle, ask him to cut off the top half, shuffle it and place it in front of himself. Then ask him to shuffle the bottom half and place it in front of you.

He can pick *X*'s or *O*'s for himself. Say he picks *O*'s. He draws the top card of his packet. If it is a 10 or picture card, he places it face down to one side. If it is any other card, he turns it face up. Say it is a 4. Draw an *O* in the space labeled "4" on the layout.

Now it is your turn. Deal the top card of your packet. If it is, say, a 9, draw an *X* in the space labeled "9" in the layout.

Continue taking turns. If either of you turns up a card value that has already been used, place this card aside face down. If the value is one that represents a blank space on the layout, turn it face up. Draw the appropriate symbol (*X* or *O*) on the layout. As the game continues, you must win.

RISING-CARD TRICKS

Each trick described here has a visual element that sets it apart. In the classic rising-card effect, you seem to have the ability to cause a chosen card to rise mysteriously out of the center of the pack. Early methods depended on specialized apparatus, but in recent years more streamlined techniques have been perfected. With some of the methods described in this chapter, you can even cause two different chosen cards to rise from the pack.

47. Simplex Card Rise

After a card has been chosen and lost in the deck, the magician drapes a handkerchief or paper napkin over the deck. When he snaps his fingers, the chosen card rises out of the pack. Borrowed cards may be used.

Method: When the borrowed deck is handed to you, secretly note the bottom card. This will be your key card. Say the key card is the ♠A.

Place the deck on the table. Lift off a small packet with the right hand and place this packet into the left hand. Continue transferring small packets from the top of the deck to the left hand. Ask the spectator to call stop.

When he does, show him the top card of the group in the left hand. Replace the chosen card on top of this group. Then pick up the balance of the cards from the table and drop this packet on top of the chosen card. The chosen card is now buried in the deck, but unknown to the audience, it lies directly below your key card.

The deck can be given several straight cuts by the spectator so that the chosen card appears to be really lost in the deck. Take back the deck. State that it is necessary to remove any jokers in order for the trick to work. Look through the deck, supposedly for jokers, but really to find the key card. Cut the key card to the bottom of the deck. In our example you would cut the ♠A to the bottom. The chosen card is now on top.

Hold the deck in the left hand. Drape a handkerchief or paper napkin over it. Place the right forefinger on top of the deck.

"By means of personal magnetism, I will cause your card to rise." As you speak, gently push up on the top card with the left thumb. Figure 81 is an exposed view with the handkerchief removed to show how the card is pushed up by the thumb. Figure 82 is the view seen by the audience. The illusion you want to create is that the card that rises seems to cling to the right forefinger.

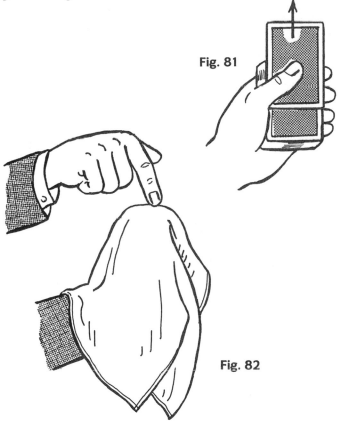

Fig. 81

Fig. 82

When the thumb has pushed up the card as far as it will go, grasp the card through the thickness of the handkerchief between the right thumb and first finger. Pull it clear of the deck. Then turn the right hand palm up, allowing the handkerchief to fall away and reveal the chosen card as shown in Figure 83.

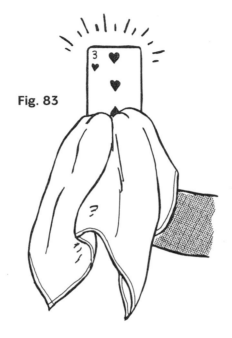

Fig. 83

48. Cards from the Case

The principle used in "Simplex Card Rise" can be applied to an effect in which the deck is dropped into the card case. The chosen card then rises from the case. Because the deck is isolated in the case, it would appear that the magician cannot control the cards. The approach described here can be used to cause two or more chosen cards (or even the four aces) to rise from the cased deck.

Method: The secret hinges on the fact that a slot has been cut in back of the case, Figure 84. In addition, with a pencil, dot the back of a joker as shown in Figure 84. The joker is placed on the bottom of the deck.

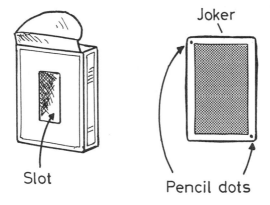

Fig. 84

When you are ready to perform the trick, place the deck on the table. Ask someone to cut the deck into three heaps. Each of three spectators then takes the top card of a heap. Ask each person to initial his card.

Place all three cards on top of the heap that has the key card at the bottom. Cut this packet and complete the cut. Place the packet on top of the next heap. Finally, place this packet on top of the third heap. Cut the deck and complete the cut.

Spread the cards face down between the hands. Say, "Your chosen cards are scattered throughout the pack." When you spot the pencil-dotted card, cut the deck at that point and complete the cut so the pencil-dotted card is on the bottom of the deck. Unknown to the audience, the three chosen cards are now on top.

"It would be easy to find your cards with the deck face up, because each of you signed your card. So let's make it harder and isolate the deck." Drop the deck into the card case so that the back of the deck is at the slotted portion of the case. Hold the case as shown in Figure 85. The left forefinger enters the slot and pushes the top card of the deck upward. Shake the cased deck back and forth as you do this. The slowly levitating card is an eerie sight. When the card has risen about halfway out of the pack, remove it with the right hand. Repeat the effect with each of the remaining chosen cards.

If you wish to produce the four aces, the preparation is as follows. Place the four aces on the table. Place the pencil-dotted

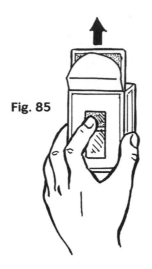

Fig. 85

joker on top of them. Drop the deck on top of all. Cut the deck and complete the cut. Then store the deck in the slotted card case. When you are ready to present this trick, remark that a gambler sent you a deck that he said always delivered the right cards. Remove the deck from the case. Place the case in your pocket. Ask the spectator to give the deck several straight cuts.

When he has done this, take back the deck. Spread the cards between the hands and say, "Of course an expert could cut to the aces if he wanted to." Spot the pencil-dotted card and cut it to the bottom of the deck. "But the gambler said the aces would produce themselves." Drop the deck into the card case. Then produce the aces by the method shown in Figure 85.

49. Excelsior Card Rise

The ingeniously simple gimmick used in this trick allows you to perform the card rise with spectators on all sides. It was invented by Stanley Palm and Rick Johnsson.

The gimmick takes less than a minute to construct. To make it, cut a joker as shown in Figure 86. The cut starts at a point about a half-inch from the upper left corner and extends to the

Cut

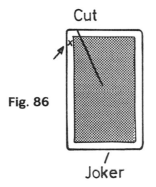

Fig. 86

Joker

center of the card. If a pair of scissors is not handy, you can carefully tear the joker to make the gimmick. Using a pen or pencil, place an *X* on the back of the card near the upper left corner so you can quickly spot the card later. The gimmicked card is placed on the bottom of the deck.

To perform the trick, place the deck on the table. Lift off the upper half, shuffle it and have a card chosen. When the card has been taken, place the packet aside.

Pick up the bottom half of the deck, cut it at the center and complete the cut. This brings the gimmick to the middle of the packet. Riffle along the left side of the packet with the left thumb, Figure 87. Stop when you spot the gimmicked card. You will hear a click when you get to the gimmicked card. That sound is made by the right side of the gimmick clicking by. Also, you will spot the *X* on the left side of the gimmick.

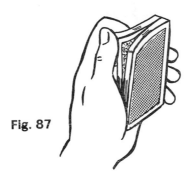

Fig. 87

The thumb holds the left side of the gimmick. Take the chosen card and insert it into the gimmick, Figure 88. An exposed view of the action is shown in Figure 89; the shaded card is the chosen card. Slide the chosen card into the packet for about half its length.

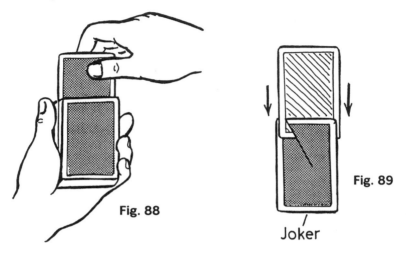

Fig. 88

Fig. 89

Joker

Grasp the packet at the right side with the right hand. This allows the left hand to pick up the card case. Insert the packet into the case so it rests in the position shown in Figure 90.

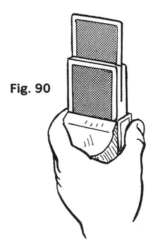

Fig. 90

Pressure at the sides of the card case by the left thumb and fingers keep the packet in place.

Push the chosen card square with the packet with the aid of the right fingers. Unknown to the audience, when the chosen card is pushed into the packet, the gimmick is pushed downward. An exposed view is shown in Figure 91.

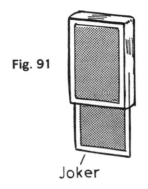

Fig. 91

Joker

Hold the apparatus as shown in Figure 92. Release pressure, allowing the packet to fall into the card case. The chosen card pops up into view, Figure 93. It is a surprising sight. Stanley Palm suggests this patter line as you release the packet: "We drop the cards *down*, and your card pops *up!*"

Fig. 92   **Fig. 93**

50. Special Delivery

Bill Severn and Pete Biro devised a clever rising-card method that has many applications. Based on a classic stage method requiring specialized apparatus, the trick has been simplified so that ordinary props are used.

Required are an envelope, a rubber band and a pencil. The envelope should be about the size shown in Figure 94. Seal the flap. Trim about 1^1/$_2$″ off one end. Then make semicircular cuts about a third of the way down from the opened end as shown in Figure 95. Finally, wrap a rubber band around the middle of the pencil as indicated in Figure 95. Put the pencil in the envelope. Place the apparatus in the pocket until the time of performance.

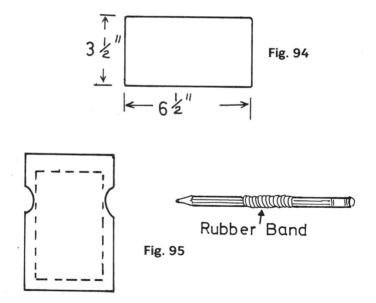

Fig. 94

Fig. 95

Rubber Band

Any deck of cards may be used. Hold the deck with the faces of the cards toward you. Say, "We will use about half the cards," as you quickly spread the cards from left to right. Remember the identity of the face card of the deck. Cut the deck at about the center. Place the lower half face down on the table. The face card of this packet is your secretly remembered key card.

Shuffle the other half of the deck. Spread the cards and have two chosen. Square the packet. Drop the two chosen cards on top of the lower packet. Cut this packet at the center and complete the cut. This brings the key card to a position directly above the two chosen cards.

Drop the upper packet on top. Cut the deck at the midpoint and complete the cut. Then cut the deck at the midpoint one more time and complete the cut.

"I ordered a pencil from a magic shop. It arrived in the mail the other day." Remove the envelope from the pocket. Then dump out the pencil. "This isn't just any pencil. Inside it is a magic wand. It makes objects float."

Pick up the deck. Hold it so you can see the faces of the cards. Beginning at the face, spread the cards from left to right. Stop when you get to the key card. Remove all of the cards in front of the key card. This is a group of about 13 cards. The top two cards of this group are the chosen cards. Place the balance of the deck to one side.

Slide the packet of cards into the envelope. Then slide the pencil through the holes in the sides of the envelope so it is above the packet. Hold the envelope in the left hand.

If you twirl the pencil in the direction of the arrow in Figure 96, the top card of the packet will rise out of the envelope. This

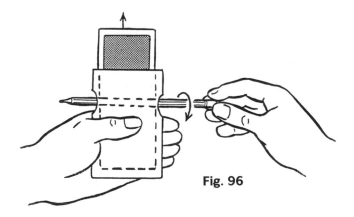

Fig. 96

is because the rubber band contacts the back of the card, causing it to move upward. If the card does not rise, the rubber band is not making contact. To correct for this, gently press against the envelope with the left thumb until the rubber band makes contact with the top card of the packet. The card will rise upward.

When the first chosen card rises into view, take it with the right hand and place it on the table. Then twirl the pencil again. The second chosen card will rise out of the envelope.

You may wish to insert the pencil into the holes in the sides of the envelope before the trick begins. This has the advantage of concealing the rubber band from audience view. Have two cards chosen as described above. When you place the packet into the envelope, slide it under the pencil. Twirl the pencil, but do it slowly, so that the motion is not obvious. Each of the chosen cards then rises mysteriously from the envelope.

An amusing variation turns an apparent mistake into success. Place the pencil into the holes in the envelope. Instead of placing the entire packet in the envelope, cut off the upper half and slide this into the envelope under the pencil. Then place the balance of the packet into the envelope over the pencil. The situation, with the envelope removed, is shown in Figure 97.

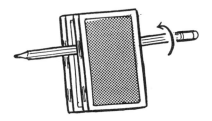

Fig. 97

Twirl the pencil in the direction of the arrow shown in Figure 97. The face card of the upper packet rises from inside the envelope. Say, "Did either of you pick this card?" Each spectator will answer no. Reverse the motion of the pencil. The wrong card sinks back, and one of the correct cards rises into view. It is a funny sight. Repeat for the second chosen card.

The author has used the following as another visual gag. Prior to performance, place the pencil in the holes in the envelope. Then place a face-up card on top of the pencil. The situation is shown in Figure 98.

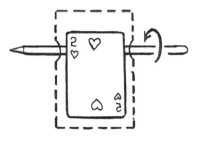

Fig. 98

Have two cards chosen as described above. The packet with the two chosen cards on top is placed into the envelope under the pencil.

Twirl the pencil in the direction of the arrow shown in Figure 98. A card will rise up out of the envelope with its back to the audience. This is the card you placed in the envelope earlier. Say, "Oops, wrong way." Reverse the direction of the pencil. The back-out card will sink into the envelope. A face-out card will rise into view. It looks as if the card somehow turned itself around.

Remove the card and place it on the table. Repeat the handling of the above paragraph. A back-out card will rise into view, then sink down, seemingly turn itself around and rise face outward. It is the other chosen card.

THE COLOR-CHANGING DECK

A modern classic that has intrigued magicians is the color-changing deck. The trick is one in which the magician starts out with a blue-backed deck and the cards magically become red-backed. This effect, originated by William McGrew, is visually one of the strongest magical tricks with cards. Decks with contrasting backs can be obtained in department stores. In each of these tricks it is assumed that the change is from blue to red because the change from dark to light is the most dramatic.

51. Reverse Colors

Rufus Steele wrote of this routine, "One of the most beautiful of card effects is that in which the backs of an entire deck appear to change color. Of the many versions which have been devised, the following is probably the most simple and direct in action." It was invented by Bob Lotz.

The magician shows a card from a red-backed deck to be the ♦2. He inserts it into a blue-backed deck. Immediately the deck becomes red-backed and the ♦2 blue-backed.

Method: Place the red-backed ♦2 in an envelope. Put the blue-backed ♦2 on top of the red-backed deck and place the deck in a blue card case. The apparatus may be kept in the pocket until the time of performance.

Remark that someone sent you a playing card that has such odd and mysterious properties, it must be kept isolated from other cards. Remove the envelope from the pocket and toss it onto the table.

"I'll show you what happens." Take the cased deck from the pocket. Remove the deck from the case, but do so with the deck face up. This way you will not accidentally flash the red-backed cards.

Hold the deck face up in the left hand, near one end. You are apparently going to show a number of blue-backed cards. Lift off ten or 12 cards from the face of the deck with the right hand, Figure 99. Place this packet on the table. Turn the left hand palm down and point to the packet, Figure 100. "Cards are printed with special quick-drying ink."

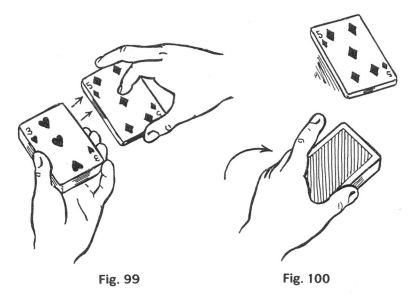

Fig. 99   Fig. 100

Turn the left hand palm up. Take another group of ten or 12 cards off the face and place them on the table. Then turn the left hand palm down and point to the packet. "After the cards are printed, they are plastic coated."

Repeat the process one more time. The idea is that by turning the left hand palm down each time, the spectators think they are seeing blue-backed cards from different parts of the pack. Actually, they are seeing the same card each time.

Gather all of the face-up cards from the table and return them to the face of the deck. Turn the deck over end for end and place it face down on the table. A blue-backed card shows on top of the deck.

"The ink can last a long time. But sometimes a wild card like this one comes along." Remove the red-backed ♦2 from the envelope. Show it on both sides. "It's red on the face and red on the back." Hold the deck steady while you slide the ♦2 into the center of the deck, Figure 101.

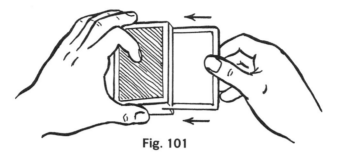

Fig. 101

Square up the deck. Turn it end for end so it is face up. Lift off about three-quarters of the deck and place it on the table. Then place the balance of the deck on top to complete the cut. Beginning at the face, spread the cards from left to right. When you get to the first ♦2, remove it from the deck and place it on the table.

"When we put the red ♦2 into the deck, all of the blue ink goes into the ♦2." Turn the ♦2 face down to show that it is blue-backed.

"And all of the red ink goes onto the deck." Turn the deck face down and spread it on the table to show that the deck is now red-backed.

52. Chemical Reaction

In this offbeat routine, only one card changes the color of its back. Seven cards are dealt to the table from a blue-backed deck. The spectator eliminates six of these. The spectator holds the chosen card between his palms. The heat from his hands causes a chemical reaction. When the card is turned over, it has changed to a red-backed card. This clever routine was devised by Arthur Carter.

Method: The cards used in this trick are the ♠A, ♦3, ♣2, ♠4, ♥6, ♣7 and the ♥5. The ♥5 is red-backed. All other cards are blue-backed. They are kept at the bottom of a blue-backed deck until the time of performance.

Hold the deck face up. Deal the seven face cards into two rows as shown in Figure 102. The precise order of the cards does not matter.

Fig. 102

"We have some red cards and some black cards. Which color shall we start with?" If the spectator says black, turn each of the black cards face down. If he names red, say, "Very well. We will use the red cards." Turn the black cards face down. In either case, you have eliminated the black cards.

"Choose either high or low." If the spectator chooses high, say, "We will use the high cards—the 5 and 6." Turn the ♦3 face down. This leaves the ♥5 and ♥6 face up.

If the spectator names low, say, "We'll use the low cards— the 3 and the 5." Turn the ♥6 face down. The ♦3 and ♥5 are face up. It can be seen that, no matter what the spectator chooses, the ♥5 will always be one of the cards remaining in play.

You will now use a line suggested by George Blake to have the spectator end up with the ♥5. Say to him, "Of the two cards remaining, would you choose one for me?"

If the spectator names the ♦3, say, "The ♦3 is for me, leaving the ♥5 for you." Turn the ♦3 face down. The ♥5 will be the only face-up card on the table. If the spectator names the ♥5, say, "Very well, we will use the ♥5." Turn the ♦3 face down. Either way you have logically arrived at the ♥5.

"By a process of following your intuition, you have arrived at the ♥5. If this is indeed your lucky card, the chemistry has to be right between you. Let's find out." Have the spectator extend one hand palm up. Place the ♥5 on his palm face up. Tell him to put his other hand palm down on top of the ♥5.

"It takes five seconds for the heat from your hand to bring about a chemical reaction." Glance at your watch. When five seconds have elapsed, have the spectator turn the ♥5 face down. The chemical reaction worked; the card now has a red back.

53. The Red and the Blue

Alex Elmsley invented an ingenious two-deck version of the color-changing deck. Each deck changes color except for a card of opposite color. These two cards are two previously chosen cards.

Method: Place a blue-backed ♣2 on top of a red deck. Put this deck into a blue card case. Place the red-backed ♣2 on top of the blue deck. Put this deck into a red card case.

As you show the two cased decks, ask the spectator to pick one. Suppose he picks the red deck. Say, "Red? Is red one of your favorite colors?" The reason for pointing up his choice is so that the audience remembers the color of the spectator's deck.

Remove the decks from their cases as you talk. Place them face down on the table. Put the spectator's chosen deck (assumed to be red) face up in front of the spectator. Put the red card case near the deck. The red case is a visual reminder of the color chosen by the spectator.

Place the blue deck face up in front of you. "I'll take the blue deck." Cut the face-up deck at the center and complete the cut.

"Do just what I do. Spread your cards on the table." The spectator spreads his deck. You spread the other deck. "Make sure you can see all the cards. We're each going to pick a card and slide it out of the spread."

Slide the ♣2 out of the center of your deck. "I'll take this card." The spectator might choose the ♥A. Take his ♥A and drop it face up on the face of your deck.

"You take my card and place it on your deck." Show the ♣2 back and front. Say, "A blue card goes into the red deck." The spectator places the ♣2 on the face of his deck.

Each of you gathers your deck. "Square up your cards like this." Square your deck, keeping it face up. The spectator does the same thing with his deck.

"Now cut the deck in the middle and complete the cut." Each of you gives his deck a straight cut.

"You picked the red deck, but watch!" Snap your fingers. Turn your deck face down. Keep it squared. "Now I have the red deck."

The spectator will turn his deck over. He has the blue deck. Say, "Remember that blue ♣2 I put in your deck?" Have the spectator spread his deck face down. There will be a red-backed card in the middle. He takes it out and turns it over; it is your ♣2, but now it has a red back.

"You put a red-backed card in my deck." Spread your cards. There will be a blue-backed card in the middle. Take it out and turn it over as you say, "Now your card has a blue back."

There are two strong points in this routine. The first is that you are apparently able to change the color of the spectator's freely chosen card, a card you could not possibly have known he would choose. The second point is that the spectator sees the back of the ♣2 you hand him. That card changes color while it is in his possession. These points make this trick especially baffling, even to magicians.

54. The Forgetful Gambler

This routine packs a triple punch. Telling the story of an absent-minded gambler, the magician mixes face-up and face-down cards in a hopeless jumble. With a snap of the fingers, the magician causes the cards to right themselves so that all cards are face up except for five face-down cards scattered in the deck. These are removed and turned face up. The five cards form a royal flush. The gambler would win with this hand, but he used the wrong magic spell. The royal flush is blue-backed, but the deck changed color and is now red-backed.

Method: This is a simplified handling of a baffling and entertaining routine developed by Bill Simon and Bill Miesel. You will need a red-backed deck, a blue-backed royal flush and a quarter. The setup from the top down is as follows: blue-backed ♦A and ♦K, face down, then 12 red-backed cards, face up, then the blue-backed ♦Q, ♦J, ♦10, face down, then the balance of the red-backed deck face down. The setup is shown in Figure 103. To complete the preparation, place the coin between the ♦10 and ♦J. Put the deck in a blue card case until the time of performance. Because of the added thickness caused by the five royal flush cards and the coin, it may be necessary to discard a few red-backed cards from the bottom of the deck so the deck will fit easily into the card case.

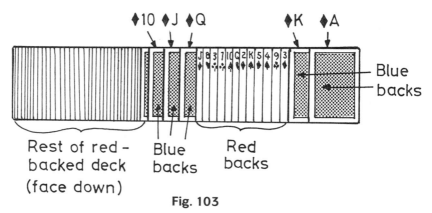

Fig. 103

"This is the story of an absentminded gambler." Remove the deck from the card case. Hold it face down in the left hand. "He was going to shuffle the deck for a game of poker, but his mind wasn't on what he was doing." Lift off all of the cards above the coin, Figure 104. This is easy to do because the coin causes a gap or separation in the deck. Simply lift off all of the cards above the gap. Place this packet on the table to the right.

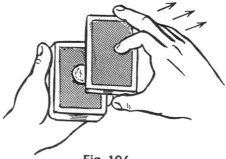

Fig. 104

"Here's the money he bet on the game, a rare coin worth *at least* 25 cents." Place the quarter on the table.

The front end of the large packet in the left hand is grasped by the right hand, Figure 105. Turn the deck over end for end and place it back into the left hand. The packet is now face up. Cut off about ten cards and place them to the left of the first packet on the table.

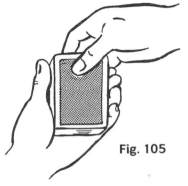

Fig. 105

Lift off about ten cards from the face of the packet in the left hand and place this packet in position *A* on the table as shown in Figure 106. Turn over the remainder of the deck end for end so it is face down. Place it at position *B* in Figure 106.

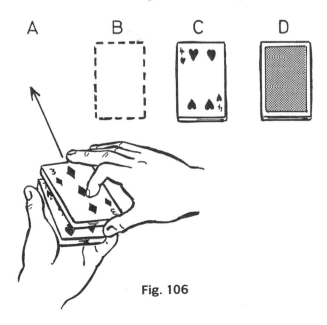

Fig. 106

"Instead of mixing the cards in the usual way, he got them all turned around." Lift off the top card of the packet at position *D* with the right hand. One way to do this without the cards accidentally spreading is as follows: place the right forefinger on top of the packet at the center of the top card. Press down on the top card to keep it in place. Lift the inner edge of the top card with the right thumb. Then grasp this card with the thumb and middle finger.

At the same time, grasp the packet at *C* by the ends with the left hand. Slip this packet between the top card at *D* and the balance of that packet. This is shown in Figure 107. It looks as if a face-up packet is going into a face-down packet.

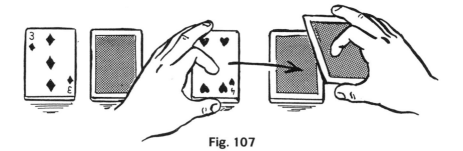

Fig. 107

"The cards really got jumbled up." Pick up the combined packet at *D*, turn it end for end and place it back on the table. The ♦J will show at the face of this packet. Pick up the packet at *B* and put it on top of the large packet.

Turn this combined packet over. Pick up the packet at *A* and place it on top. The deck has now been assembled.

"The gambler realized his mistake. But he claimed he knew a way to cause all the cards to face the same way." Grasp the deck by the ends with the right hand. Slide out the backmost card with the left fingers, Figure 108. This card will be the ♦10. Turn this card face down. Wave it over the deck.

"He tried to say the magic words, but he got them mixed up. The best he could do was 'hocus rebus, jokus pokus.' "

Place the face-down ♦10 on the table. Spread the deck face up from left to right on the table. The first surprise comes in at this point. The audience thinks that face-up and face-down cards are hopelessly mixed. But when the deck is spread, most of the cards are face up.

Fig. 108

"Well, it almost worked." Point to the few face-down cards in the deck. "He said he might as well take these cards as his poker hand." Beginning at the far left, remove the face-down cards one at a time and place them on top of the ♦10. When this has been done, square up the deck but keep it face up.

"Here's the hand he got." The second surprise happens now. Deal the five blue-backed cards in a face-up row on the table to reveal a royal flush.

"It looked like he would win the game. After all, nothing beats a royal flush." Turn the royal flush face down. You want the blue backs to show.

"But being absentminded, he didn't realize that the magic spell had a surprising effect. These cards are blue-backed." Point to the royal flush.

"But these cards are not." Turn the deck face down and spread it on the table. The appearance of the red backs is a surprising finish to the routine.

55. 52-Card Monte

The color-changing deck is used here as a surprise ending to a comedy version of the swindler's game of three-card monte. In the classic swindle, the spectator cannot pick out the ace, despite his best efforts. In this routine he has no trouble finding the ace, despite the magician's best efforts. The trick was invented by the author.

Method: Cut the ♠A to the bottom of a red-backed deck. On top of the deck stack the blue-backed ♥Q, ♦Q and ♠A in that order, the ♥Q being the top card of the deck. Place the deck in a blue card case until the time of performance.

"Last week I met the best gambler in town. He showed me the real secret of the game known as three-card monte." As you speak, remove the deck from the case. Point to the face card of the deck, the ♠A. "Try to follow the ace as I do the moves."

Grasp the deck from above with the right hand, Figure 109, and slap it face down on the table. "Okay, where do you think the ace is?"

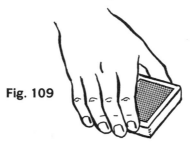

Fig. 109

The spectator will point to the deck (where else can he point?). Pause for a long moment as if puzzled. "Talk about beginner's luck. You guessed right this time." Grasp the deck from above with the right hand, turn it face up to show the ♠A at the face, then turn the deck face down and replace it on the table.

Pretend you have figured out your mistake. "Of course. I should have used two cards. No wonder it was so easy for you." Remove the top card, show it to be the ♥Q and place it face down on the table.

Grasp the deck from above with one hand, the ♥Q with the other. Cross the hands and place the cards on the table. "*Now* let's see you find the ♠A." Of course the spectator will point to the deck. Act amazed. "You must be the luckiest man alive." Grasp the deck from above. Turn it face up and show the ♠A on the face. Put the deck face down on the table.

Snap the fingers as if finally seeing your mistake. "Now I remember. This game is called *three*-card monte for a reason. Here I've been using two cards." Lift off the top card, show it to be the other red queen and place it face down on the table.

Pick up the deck from above and slap it down on the table. Pick up a queen in each hand. Toss the one from the right hand to the left of the deck and the one in the left hand to the right of the deck.

"I *challenge* you to find the ace now." The spectator points to the deck. Grasp the deck from above, turn it face up and show the ♠A at the face. Keep the deck face up because there is a surprise ending coming up.

"I'm beginning to think you took lessons from the same gambler. In fact, you dress like him—white shirt, red tie." (You merely describe what the spectator is wearing.)

"I'll offer you double or nothing. Find the ace now." As you speak, cut the deck and complete the cut. Spread the deck face down on the table. The deck, believed to be blue-backed, has suddenly changed color. When the spectator gets over that surprise, he notices a blue-backed card in the middle of the deck. Of course he will point to that card.

Ignore the fact that this card has an odd-color back. Turn it face up to show the ♠A and say, "You found it again. How did you do it?"

GUESSING THE COLORS

Sometimes a card trick has a profound effect out of proportion to the means you employ. The trick that is the subject of this chapter is just such an example. During World War II, some of Winston Churchill's friends arranged a dinner party to divert the mind of England's Prime Minister from the burdens of the war. When the dinner was over, magician Harry Green performed an amazing new card trick for Mr. Churchill and his guests. Astonished by this trick, Churchill asked to see it performed again. And again he was baffled. The trick was repeated six times in all. Churchill finally had to leave to address Parliament. Reporting on the incident, the London *Times* said that Mr. Churchill arrived at Parliament at 2 A.M. looking "befogged."

This trick, a modern-day classic invented by Paul Curry, is the subject of this chapter.

56. Out of This World

The effect is one in which the spectator, asked to guess the color of each card in the deck, is amazed to learn that, purely by guesswork, he has correctly guessed the color of *every* card. The spectator's choice is in no way influenced by the magician, and the cards are ordinary. This is a streamlined handling of the original trick.

Method: You will need two glasses or coffee mugs, each large enough to hold about half the deck. Four pieces of cardboard are also used. They are each as wide as a playing card and about 4½" high.

On one card write "Red" on both sides near one end. On a second card write "Black" on both sides near one end. These cards are shown in Figures 110 and 111.

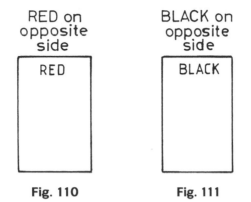

RED on opposite side

RED

BLACK on opposite side

BLACK

Fig. 110   **Fig. 111**

On each side of the other two cards, near one end, write "Red" on one side, "Black" on the other. These cards are shown in Figures 112 and 113.

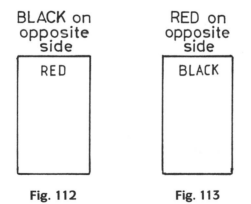

BLACK on opposite side

RED

RED on opposite side

BLACK

Fig. 112   **Fig. 113**

Place the card from Figure 110 in one mug. Place the card from Figure 113 in the second mug. See Figure 114 for the audience's view of the apparatus. The second mug is shown shaded in the drawings so that the handling will be easier to follow.

The deck is stacked so the red cards are on top, the black cards on the bottom. The twenty-sixth card from the top of the

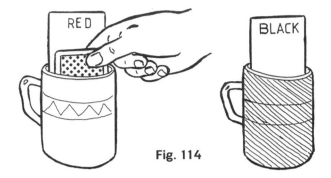

Fig. 114

deck is dotted with a pencil or otherwise secretly marked so you can spot it at a glance. The mugs, the deck of cards and the pieces of cardboard can be kept on a tray until the time of performance.

To present the routine, explain to your guests that you would like to try an experiment in clairvoyance. This is the ability to see things hidden from ordinary sight. Remove the deck of cards from its case. Hand the top quarter of the deck to one spectator, the next quarter (up to and including the pencil-dotted card) to a second spectator, the next quarter to a third spectator and the last quarter to yet another spectator.

Ask each person to shuffle his or her cards. Caution each person to keep the cards face down so there can be no clue as to their order.

After the cards have been mixed, take back the last quarter. Cut it in half and complete the cut. Take back the next quarter, give it a straight cut and combine it with the cards in hand. Unknown to the audience, this combined packet contains only black cards. Take back the next quarter. This is the one that contains the pencil-dotted card. Cut it at the pencil-dotted card and complete the cut so the pencil-dotted card is at the bottom of this packet. Place the packet on top of the black cards. Take back the remaining quarter of the deck. Give it a cut and drop it on top of the other cards. The deck has now been assembled.

Ask a spectator to guess the color of each card. Take the top card of the deck. Keep the face of the card hidden from the audience. If the spectator guesses that this card is red, put the card into the mug with the "Red" cardboard, Figure 114. If he guesses black, put it into the other mug.

Continue this way until you have gone through 26 cards.

The pencil-dotted card is the last card this spectator will guess. When you have only the black cards in your hand, say, "We'll let another spectator try his hand with the remaining cards." Put the cardboard shown in Figure 111 into the mug on the left, the cardboard shown in Figure 112 into the shaded mug. The apparatus now looks as shown in Figure 115.

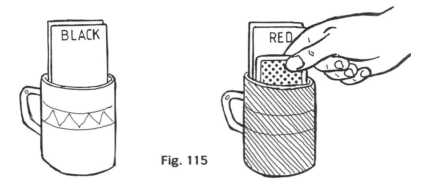

Fig. 115

Ask a second spectator to guess the colors of the remaining cards. If he says a card is red, put it into the shaded mug, Figure 115. If he says the card is black, put it into the other mug. Continue until all of the cards have been placed in the mugs.

"Let's see how well you did."

Grasp the cards in the shaded mug. The performer is standing behind the apparatus. His view of this action is shown in Figure 116. Remove all of the cards and the two pieces of cardboard together as indicated in Figure 117.

Performer's View

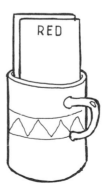

Fig. 116

Fig. 117

Ask a nearby spectator to remove all of the cards from the other mug. As he does this, lower your packet so it is horizontal, that is, parallel to the floor. Place it in the left hand as shown in Figure 118. Spread your cards from hand to hand, Figure 119. The cardboard at the face of the packet (the one that shows the word "Red") is placed on the table to the right. Place all of the red cards, squared up, near this cardboard. Say, "It looks as if you did better than average."

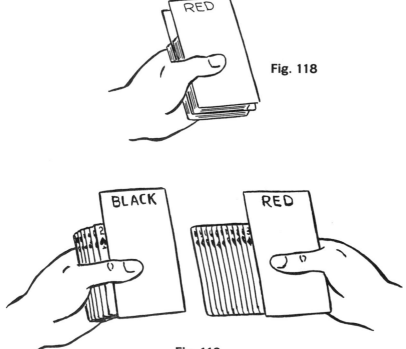

Fig. 118

Fig. 119

The piece of cardboard with "Black" showing is placed on the table to the left. Place the remainder of your cards in a squared heap near this cardboard.

"Let's check your score." Pick up the two pieces of cardboard and put them in your pocket as if to get them out of the way. Spread the red packet, showing all red cards. Spread the black packet, showing all black cards. "This is amazing. It's the first time anyone has gotten a perfect score with this many cards. Let's see how well you did with the rest of the deck."

The spectator examines the cards in the other half of the deck. The audience will be astonished to discover that these cards also show a perfect score. Finish by saying, "I wouldn't want to play cards with you!"

There are a number of touches you can add to the routine that will make it more effective. First, remove three red and three black cards from the deck. Arrange the rest of the deck so the reds are on top, the blacks on the bottom. Pencil-dot the red card that lies twenty-third from the top of the deck. Shuffle the six cards you removed from the deck so the colors are mixed. Place them on the top of the deck.

When you remove the deck from the case, deal the first six cards off the top. Turn them face up as you deal them, and openly separate them into two heaps, one red and the other black. Say, "It's easy to separate the colors if we look at the faces of the cards." When you have dealt the six cards off, place them aside. "It's harder to do it accurately if we don't look at the faces of the cards." Proceed from here with the trick as described above. The fact that the audience sees a mixture of reds and blacks in the first six cards implies that the colors are well mixed throughout the rest of the deck.

Another suggestion is to place a small "X" on the backs of two jokers. Place one joker among the blacks, the other joker among the reds. Do the trick as described, but when you get to the X'd card in the top half of the deck, pause when the spectator guesses the color of this card. Say, "You seemed to hesitate on this card. Are you *sure* you guessed right?" Whatever his reply, show that the card is the joker. "Of course. This card isn't red or black." Toss it aside. Repeat with the other joker when you get to it.

You can have two ungimmicked pieces of cardboard in the pocket, that is, one which shows "Red" on both sides, one which shows "Black" on both sides. After the conclusion of the trick, should anyone ask to see the pieces of cardboard you put in your pocket, you can bring out these two pieces of cardboard.

When performing the routine, encourage each spectator, telling them they are doing better than average. Stop every once in a while to ask if the person wants to change his mind about a particular guess. Try to strike a balance between enthusiasm and doubt, so that you can give the appearance you are not sure of the outcome but think it is going to be far better than average. Then act amazed that a perfect score was achieved.

A CATALOG OF SELECTED
DOVER BOOKS
IN ALL FIELDS OF INTEREST

A CATALOG OF SELECTED DOVER
BOOKS IN ALL FIELDS OF INTEREST

CONCERNING THE SPIRITUAL IN ART, Wassily Kandinsky. Pioneering work by father of abstract art. Thoughts on color theory, nature of art. Analysis of earlier masters. 12 illustrations. 80pp. of text. 5⅜ x 8½. 23411-8 Pa. $3.95

ANIMALS: 1,419 Copyright-Free Illustrations of Mammals, Birds, Fish, Insects, etc., Jim Harter (ed.). Clear wood engravings present, in extremely lifelike poses, over 1,000 species of animals. One of the most extensive pictorial sourcebooks of its kind. Captions. Index. 284pp. 9 x 12. 23766-4 Pa. $12.95

CELTIC ART: The Methods of Construction, George Bain. Simple geometric techniques for making Celtic interlacements, spirals, Kells-type initials, animals, humans, etc. Over 500 illustrations. 160pp. 9 x 12. (USO) 22923-8 Pa. $9.95

AN ATLAS OF ANATOMY FOR ARTISTS, Fritz Schider. Most thorough reference work on art anatomy in the world. Hundreds of illustrations, including selections from works by Vesalius, Leonardo, Goya, Ingres, Michelangelo, others. 593 illustrations. 192pp. 7⅛ x 10¼. 20241-0 Pa. $9.95

CELTIC HAND STROKE-BY-STROKE (Irish Half-Uncial from "The Book of Kells"): An Arthur Baker Calligraphy Manual, Arthur Baker. Complete guide to creating each letter of the alphabet in distinctive Celtic manner. Covers hand position, strokes, pens, inks, paper, more. Illustrated. 48pp. 8¼ x 11. 24336-2 Pa. $3.95

EASY ORIGAMI, John Montroll. Charming collection of 32 projects (hat, cup, pelican, piano, swan, many more) specially designed for the novice origami hobbyist. Clearly illustrated easy-to-follow instructions insure that even beginning papercrafters will achieve successful results. 48pp. 8¼ x 11. 27298-2 Pa. $3.50

THE COMPLETE BOOK OF BIRDHOUSE CONSTRUCTION FOR WOOD-WORKERS, Scott D. Campbell. Detailed instructions, illustrations, tables. Also data on bird habitat and instinct patterns. Bibliography. 3 tables. 63 illustrations in 15 figures. 48pp. 5¼ x 8½. 24407-5 Pa. $2.50

BLOOMINGDALE'S ILLUSTRATED 1886 CATALOG: Fashions, Dry Goods and Housewares, Bloomingdale Brothers. Famed merchants' extremely rare catalog depicting about 1,700 products: clothing, housewares, firearms, dry goods, jewelry, more. Invaluable for dating, identifying vintage items. Also, copyright-free graphics for artists, designers. Co-published with Henry Ford Museum & Greenfield Village. 160pp. 8¼ x 11. 25780-0 Pa. $10.95

HISTORIC COSTUME IN PICTURES, Braun & Schneider. Over 1,450 costumed figures in clearly detailed engravings–from dawn of civilization to end of 19th century. Captions. Many folk costumes. 256pp. 8⅜ x 11¾. 23150-X Pa. $12.95

STICKLEY CRAFTSMAN FURNITURE CATALOGS, Gustav Stickley and L. & J. G. Stickley. Beautiful, functional furniture in two authentic catalogs from 1910. 594 illustrations, including 277 photos, show settles, rockers, armchairs, reclining chairs, bookcases, desks, tables. 183pp. 6½ x 9¼. 23838-5 Pa. $9.95

AMERICAN LOCOMOTIVES IN HISTORIC PHOTOGRAPHS: 1858 to 1949, Ron Ziel (ed.). A rare collection of 126 meticulously detailed official photographs, called "builder portraits," of American locomotives that majestically chronicle the rise of steam locomotive power in America. Introduction. Detailed captions. xi + 129pp. 9 x 12. 27393-8 Pa. $12.95

AMERICA'S LIGHTHOUSES: An Illustrated History, Francis Ross Holland, Jr. Delightfully written, profusely illustrated fact-filled survey of over 200 American lighthouses since 1716. History, anecdotes, technological advances, more. 240pp. 8 x 10¾. 25576-X Pa. $12.95

TOWARDS A NEW ARCHITECTURE, Le Corbusier. Pioneering manifesto by founder of "International School." Technical and aesthetic theories, views of industry, economics, relation of form to function, "mass-production split" and much more. Profusely illustrated. 320pp. 6⅛ x 9¼. (USO) 25023-7 Pa. $9.95

HOW THE OTHER HALF LIVES, Jacob Riis. Famous journalistic record, exposing poverty and degradation of New York slums around 1900, by major social reformer. 100 striking and influential photographs. 233pp. 10 x 7⅞. 22012-5 Pa. $10.95

FRUIT KEY AND TWIG KEY TO TREES AND SHRUBS, William M. Harlow. One of the handiest and most widely used identification aids. Fruit key covers 120 deciduous and evergreen species; twig key 160 deciduous species. Easily used. Over 300 photographs. 126pp. 5⅜ x 8½. 20511-8 Pa. $3.95

COMMON BIRD SONGS, Dr. Donald J. Borror. Songs of 60 most common U.S. birds: robins, sparrows, cardinals, bluejays, finches, more–arranged in order of increasing complexity. Up to 9 variations of songs of each species.
Cassette and manual 99911-4 $8.95

ORCHIDS AS HOUSE PLANTS, Rebecca Tyson Northen. Grow cattleyas and many other kinds of orchids–in a window, in a case, or under artificial light. 63 illustrations. 148pp. 5⅜ x 8½. 23261-1 Pa. $4.95

MONSTER MAZES, Dave Phillips. Masterful mazes at four levels of difficulty. Avoid deadly perils and evil creatures to find magical treasures. Solutions for all 32 exciting illustrated puzzles. 48pp. 8¼ x 11. 26005-4 Pa. $2.95

MOZART'S DON GIOVANNI (DOVER OPERA LIBRETTO SERIES), Wolfgang Amadeus Mozart. Introduced and translated by Ellen H. Bleiler. Standard Italian libretto, with complete English translation. Convenient and thoroughly portable–an ideal companion for reading along with a recording or the performance itself. Introduction. List of characters. Plot summary. 121pp. 5¼ x 8½. 24944-1 Pa. $2.95

TECHNICAL MANUAL AND DICTIONARY OF CLASSICAL BALLET, Gail Grant. Defines, explains, comments on steps, movements, poses and concepts. 15-page pictorial section. Basic book for student, viewer. 127pp. 5⅜ x 8½. 21843-0 Pa. $4.95

BRASS INSTRUMENTS: Their History and Development, Anthony Baines. Authoritative, updated survey of the evolution of trumpets, trombones, bugles, cornets, French horns, tubas and other brass wind instruments. Over 140 illustrations and 48 music examples. Corrected and updated by author. New preface. Bibliography. 320pp. 5⅜ x 8½. 27574-4 Pa. $9.95

HOLLYWOOD GLAMOR PORTRAITS, John Kobal (ed.). 145 photos from 1926-49. Harlow, Gable, Bogart, Bacall; 94 stars in all. Full background on photographers, technical aspects. 160pp. 8⅜ x 11¼. 23352-9 Pa. $12.95

MAX AND MORITZ, Wilhelm Busch. Great humor classic in both German and English. Also 10 other works: "Cat and Mouse," "Plisch and Plumm," etc. 216pp. 5⅜ x 8½. 20181-3 Pa. $6.95

THE RAVEN AND OTHER FAVORITE POEMS, Edgar Allan Poe. Over 40 of the author's most memorable poems: "The Bells," "Ulalume," "Israfel," "To Helen," "The Conqueror Worm," "Eldorado," "Annabel Lee," many more. Alphabetic lists of titles and first lines. 64pp. 5³⁄₁₆ x 8¼. 26685-0 Pa. $1.00

PERSONAL MEMOIRS OF U. S. GRANT, Ulysses Simpson Grant. Intelligent, deeply moving firsthand account of Civil War campaigns, considered by many the finest military memoirs ever written. Includes letters, historic photographs, maps and more. 528pp. 6⅛ x 9¼. 28587-1 Pa. $11.95

AMULETS AND SUPERSTITIONS, E. A. Wallis Budge. Comprehensive discourse on origin, powers of amulets in many ancient cultures: Arab, Persian Babylonian, Assyrian, Egyptian, Gnostic, Hebrew, Phoenician, Syriac, etc. Covers cross, swastika, crucifix, seals, rings, stones, etc. 584pp. 5⅜ x 8½. 23573-4 Pa. $12.95

RUSSIAN STORIES/PYCCKNE PACCKA3bl: A Dual-Language Book, edited by Gleb Struve. Twelve tales by such masters as Chekhov, Tolstoy, Dostoevsky, Pushkin, others. Excellent word-for-word English translations on facing pages, plus teaching and study aids, Russian/English vocabulary, biographical/critical introductions, more. 416pp. 5⅜ x 8½. 26244-8 Pa. $8.95

PHILADELPHIA THEN AND NOW: 60 Sites Photographed in the Past and Present, Kenneth Finkel and Susan Oyama. Rare photographs of City Hall, Logan Square, Independence Hall, Betsy Ross House, other landmarks juxtaposed with contemporary views. Captures changing face of historic city. Introduction. Captions. 128pp. 8¼ x 11. 25790-8 Pa. $9.95

AIA ARCHITECTURAL GUIDE TO NASSAU AND SUFFOLK COUNTIES, LONG ISLAND, The American Institute of Architects, Long Island Chapter, and the Society for the Preservation of Long Island Antiquities. Comprehensive, well-researched and generously illustrated volume brings to life over three centuries of Long Island's great architectural heritage. More than 240 photographs with authoritative, extensively detailed captions. 176pp. 8¼ x 11. 26946-9 Pa. $14.95

NORTH AMERICAN INDIAN LIFE: Customs and Traditions of 23 Tribes, Elsie Clews Parsons (ed.). 27 fictionalized essays by noted anthropologists examine religion, customs, government, additional facets of life among the Winnebago, Crow, Zuni, Eskimo, other tribes. 480pp. 6⅛ x 9¼. 27377-6 Pa. $10.95

FRANK LLOYD WRIGHT'S HOLLYHOCK HOUSE, Donald Hoffmann. Lavishly illustrated, carefully documented study of one of Wright's most controversial residential designs. Over 120 photographs, floor plans, elevations, etc. Detailed perceptive text by noted Wright scholar. Index. 128pp. 9¼ x 10¾. 27133-1 Pa. $11.95

THE MALE AND FEMALE FIGURE IN MOTION: 60 Classic Photographic Sequences, Eadweard Muybridge. 60 true-action photographs of men and women walking, running, climbing, bending, turning, etc., reproduced from rare 19th-century masterpiece. vi + 121pp. 9 x 12. 24745-7 Pa. $10.95

1001 QUESTIONS ANSWERED ABOUT THE SEASHORE, N. J. Berrill and Jacquelyn Berrill. Queries answered about dolphins, sea snails, sponges, starfish, fishes, shore birds, many others. Covers appearance, breeding, growth, feeding, much more. 305pp. 5¼ x 8¼. 23366-9 Pa. $8.95

GUIDE TO OWL WATCHING IN NORTH AMERICA, Donald S. Heintzelman. Superb guide offers complete data and descriptions of 19 species: barn owl, screech owl, snowy owl, many more. Expert coverage of owl-watching equipment, conservation, migrations and invasions, etc. Guide to observing sites. 84 illustrations. xiii + 193pp. 5⅜ x 8½. 27344-X Pa. $8.95

MEDICINAL AND OTHER USES OF NORTH AMERICAN PLANTS: A Historical Survey with Special Reference to the Eastern Indian Tribes, Charlotte Erichsen-Brown. Chronological historical citations document 500 years of usage of plants, trees, shrubs native to eastern Canada, northeastern U.S. Also complete identifying information. 343 illustrations. 544pp. 6½ x 9¼. 25951-X Pa. $12.95

STORYBOOK MAZES, Dave Phillips. 23 stories and mazes on two-page spreads: Wizard of Oz, Treasure Island, Robin Hood, etc. Solutions. 64pp. 8¼ x 11. 23628-5 Pa. $2.95

NEGRO FOLK MUSIC, U.S.A., Harold Courlander. Noted folklorist's scholarly yet readable analysis of rich and varied musical tradition. Includes authentic versions of over 40 folk songs. Valuable bibliography and discography. xi + 324pp. 5⅜ x 8½. 27350-4 Pa. $9.95

MOVIE-STAR PORTRAITS OF THE FORTIES, John Kobal (ed.). 163 glamor, studio photos of 106 stars of the 1940s: Rita Hayworth, Ava Gardner, Marlon Brando, Clark Gable, many more. 176pp. 8⅝ x 11¼. 23546-7 Pa. $12.95

BENCHLEY LOST AND FOUND, Robert Benchley. Finest humor from early 30s, about pet peeves, child psychologists, post office and others. Mostly unavailable elsewhere. 73 illustrations by Peter Arno and others. 183pp. 5⅜ x 8½. 22410-4 Pa. $6.95

YEKL and THE IMPORTED BRIDEGROOM AND OTHER STORIES OF YIDDISH NEW YORK, Abraham Cahan. Film Hester Street based on Yekl (1896). Novel, other stories among first about Jewish immigrants on N.Y.'s East Side. 240pp. 5⅜ x 8½. 22427-9 Pa. $6.95

SELECTED POEMS, Walt Whitman. Generous sampling from *Leaves of Grass*. Twenty-four poems include "I Hear America Singing," "Song of the Open Road," "I Sing the Body Electric," "When Lilacs Last in the Dooryard Bloom'd," "O Captain! My Captain!"–all reprinted from an authoritative edition. Lists of titles and first lines. 128pp. 5³⁄₁₆ x 8¼. 26878-0 Pa. $1.00

THE BEST TALES OF HOFFMANN, E. T. A. Hoffmann. 10 of Hoffmann's most important stories: "Nutcracker and the King of Mice," "The Golden Flowerpot," etc. 458pp. 5⅜ x 8½. 21793-0 Pa. $9.95

FROM FETISH TO GOD IN ANCIENT EGYPT, E. A. Wallis Budge. Rich detailed survey of Egyptian conception of "God" and gods, magic, cult of animals, Osiris, more. Also, superb English translations of hymns and legends. 240 illustrations. 545pp. 5⅜ x 8½. 25803-3 Pa. $13.95

FRENCH STORIES/CONTES FRANÇAIS: A Dual-Language Book, Wallace Fowlie. Ten stories by French masters, Voltaire to Camus: "Micromegas" by Voltaire; "The Atheist's Mass" by Balzac; "Minuet" by de Maupassant; "The Guest" by Camus, six more. Excellent English translations on facing pages. Also French-English vocabulary list, exercises, more. 352pp. 5⅜ x 8½. 26443-2 Pa. $8.95

CHICAGO AT THE TURN OF THE CENTURY IN PHOTOGRAPHS: 122 Historic Views from the Collections of the Chicago Historical Society, Larry A. Viskochil. Rare large-format prints offer detailed views of City Hall, State Street, the Loop, Hull House, Union Station, many other landmarks, circa 1904-1913. Introduction. Captions. Maps. 144pp. 9⅜ x 12¼. 24656-6 Pa. $12.95

OLD BROOKLYN IN EARLY PHOTOGRAPHS, 1865-1929, William Lee Younger. Luna Park, Gravesend race track, construction of Grand Army Plaza, moving of Hotel Brighton, etc. 157 previously unpublished photographs. 165pp. 8⅞ x 11¾. 23587-4 Pa. $13.95

THE MYTHS OF THE NORTH AMERICAN INDIANS, Lewis Spence. Rich anthology of the myths and legends of the Algonquins, Iroquois, Pawnees and Sioux, prefaced by an extensive historical and ethnological commentary. 36 illustrations. 480pp. 5⅜ x 8½. 25967-6 Pa. $8.95

AN ENCYCLOPEDIA OF BATTLES: Accounts of Over 1,560 Battles from 1479 B.C. to the Present, David Eggenberger. Essential details of every major battle in recorded history from the first battle of Megiddo in 1479 B.C. to Grenada in 1984. List of Battle Maps. New Appendix covering the years 1967-1984. Index. 99 illustrations. 544pp. 6½ x 9¼. 24913-1 Pa. $14.95

SAILING ALONE AROUND THE WORLD, Captain Joshua Slocum. First man to sail around the world, alone, in small boat. One of great feats of seamanship told in delightful manner. 67 illustrations. 294pp. 5⅜ x 8½. 20326-3 Pa. $5.95

ANARCHISM AND OTHER ESSAYS, Emma Goldman. Powerful, penetrating, prophetic essays on direct action, role of minorities, prison reform, puritan hypocrisy, violence, etc. 271pp. 5⅜ x 8½. 22484-8 Pa. $6.95

MYTHS OF THE HINDUS AND BUDDHISTS, Ananda K. Coomaraswamy and Sister Nivedita. Great stories of the epics; deeds of Krishna, Shiva, taken from puranas, Vedas, folk tales; etc. 32 illustrations. 400pp. 5⅜ x 8½. 21759-0 Pa. $10.95

BEYOND PSYCHOLOGY, Otto Rank. Fear of death, desire of immortality, nature of sexuality, social organization, creativity, according to Rankian system. 291pp. 5⅜ x 8½. 20485-5 Pa. $8.95

A THEOLOGICO-POLITICAL TREATISE, Benedict Spinoza. Also contains unfinished Political Treatise. Great classic on religious liberty, theory of government on common consent. R. Elwes translation. Total of 421pp. 5⅜ x 8½. 20249-6 Pa. $9.95

MY BONDAGE AND MY FREEDOM, Frederick Douglass. Born a slave, Douglass became outspoken force in antislavery movement. The best of Douglass' autobiographies. Graphic description of slave life. 464pp. 5⅜ x 8½. 22457-0 Pa. $8.95

FOLLOWING THE EQUATOR: A Journey Around the World, Mark Twain. Fascinating humorous account of 1897 voyage to Hawaii, Australia, India, New Zealand, etc. Ironic, bemused reports on peoples, customs, climate, flora and fauna, politics, much more. 197 illustrations. 720pp. 5⅜ x 8½. 26113-1 Pa. $15.95

THE PEOPLE CALLED SHAKERS, Edward D. Andrews. Definitive study of Shakers: origins, beliefs, practices, dances, social organization, furniture and crafts, etc. 33 illustrations. 351pp. 5⅜ x 8½. 21081-2 Pa. $8.95

THE MYTHS OF GREECE AND ROME, H. A. Guerber. A classic of mythology, generously illustrated, long prized for its simple, graphic, accurate retelling of the principal myths of Greece and Rome, and for its commentary on their origins and significance. With 64 illustrations by Michelangelo, Raphael, Titian, Rubens, Canova, Bernini and others. 480pp. 5⅜ x 8½. 27584-1 Pa. $9.95

PSYCHOLOGY OF MUSIC, Carl E. Seashore. Classic work discusses music as a medium from psychological viewpoint. Clear treatment of physical acoustics, auditory apparatus, sound perception, development of musical skills, nature of musical feeling, host of other topics. 88 figures. 408pp. 5⅜ x 8½. 21851-1 Pa. $10.95

THE PHILOSOPHY OF HISTORY, Georg W. Hegel. Great classic of Western thought develops concept that history is not chance but rational process, the evolution of freedom. 457pp. 5⅜ x 8½. 20112-0 Pa. $9.95

THE BOOK OF TEA, Kakuzo Okakura. Minor classic of the Orient: entertaining, charming explanation, interpretation of traditional Japanese culture in terms of tea ceremony. 94pp. 5⅜ x 8½. 20070-1 Pa. $3.95

LIFE IN ANCIENT EGYPT, Adolf Erman. Fullest, most thorough, detailed older account with much not in more recent books, domestic life, religion, magic, medicine, commerce, much more. Many illustrations reproduce tomb paintings, carvings, hieroglyphs, etc. 597pp. 5⅜ x 8½. 22632-8 Pa. $11.95

SUNDIALS, Their Theory and Construction, Albert Waugh. Far and away the best, most thorough coverage of ideas, mathematics concerned, types, construction, adjusting anywhere. Simple, nontechnical treatment allows even children to build several of these dials. Over 100 illustrations. 230pp. 5⅜ x 8½. 22947-5 Pa. $7.95

DYNAMICS OF FLUIDS IN POROUS MEDIA, Jacob Bear. For advanced students of ground water hydrology, soil mechanics and physics, drainage and irrigation engineering, and more. 335 illustrations. Exercises, with answers. 784pp. 6⅛ x 9¼. 65675-6 Pa. $19.95

SONGS OF EXPERIENCE: Facsimile Reproduction with 26 Plates in Full Color, William Blake. 26 full-color plates from a rare 1826 edition. Includes "TheTyger," "London," "Holy Thursday," and other poems. Printed text of poems. 48pp. 5¼ x 7. 24636-1 Pa. $4.95

OLD-TIME VIGNETTES IN FULL COLOR, Carol Belanger Grafton (ed.). Over 390 charming, often sentimental illustrations, selected from archives of Victorian graphics—pretty women posing, children playing, food, flowers, kittens and puppies, smiling cherubs, birds and butterflies, much more. All copyright-free. 48pp. 9¼ x 12¼. 27269-9 Pa. $7.95

PERSPECTIVE FOR ARTISTS, Rex Vicat Cole. Depth, perspective of sky and sea, shadows, much more, not usually covered. 391 diagrams, 81 reproductions of drawings and paintings. 279pp. 5⅜ x 8½. 22487-2 Pa. $7.95

DRAWING THE LIVING FIGURE, Joseph Sheppard. Innovative approach to artistic anatomy focuses on specifics of surface anatomy, rather than muscles and bones. Over 170 drawings of live models in front, back and side views, and in widely varying poses. Accompanying diagrams. 177 illustrations. Introduction. Index. 144pp. 8⅜ x11¼. 26723-7 Pa. $8.95

GOTHIC AND OLD ENGLISH ALPHABETS: 100 Complete Fonts, Dan X. Solo. Add power, elegance to posters, signs, other graphics with 100 stunning copyright-free alphabets: Blackstone, Dolbey, Germania, 97 more–including many lower-case, numerals, punctuation marks. 104pp. 8⅛ x 11. 24695-7 Pa. $8.95

HOW TO DO BEADWORK, Mary White. Fundamental book on craft from simple projects to five-bead chains and woven works. 106 illustrations. 142pp. 5⅜ x 8. 20697-1 Pa. $4.95

THE BOOK OF WOOD CARVING, Charles Marshall Sayers. Finest book for beginners discusses fundamentals and offers 34 designs. "Absolutely first rate . . . well thought out and well executed."–E. J. Tangerman. 118pp. 7¾ x 10⅝. 23654-4 Pa. $6.95

ILLUSTRATED CATALOG OF CIVIL WAR MILITARY GOODS: Union Army Weapons, Insignia, Uniform Accessories, and Other Equipment, Schuyler, Hartley, and Graham. Rare, profusely illustrated 1846 catalog includes Union Army uniform and dress regulations, arms and ammunition, coats, insignia, flags, swords, rifles, etc. 226 illustrations. 160pp. 9 x 12. 24939-5 Pa. $10.95

WOMEN'S FASHIONS OF THE EARLY 1900s: An Unabridged Republication of "New York Fashions, 1909," National Cloak & Suit Co. Rare catalog of mail-order fashions documents women's and children's clothing styles shortly after the turn of the century. Captions offer full descriptions, prices. Invaluable resource for fashion, costume historians. Approximately 725 illustrations. 128pp. 8⅜ x 11¼. 27276-1 Pa. $11.95

THE 1912 AND 1915 GUSTAV STICKLEY FURNITURE CATALOGS, Gustav Stickley. With over 200 detailed illustrations and descriptions, these two catalogs are essential reading and reference materials and identification guides for Stickley furniture. Captions cite materials, dimensions and prices. 112pp. 6½ x 9¼. 26676-1 Pa. $9.95

EARLY AMERICAN LOCOMOTIVES, John H. White, Jr. Finest locomotive engravings from early 19th century: historical (1804–74), main-line (after 1870), special, foreign, etc. 147 plates. 142pp. 11⅜ x 8¼. 22772-3 Pa. $10.95

THE TALL SHIPS OF TODAY IN PHOTOGRAPHS, Frank O. Braynard. Lavishly illustrated tribute to nearly 100 majestic contemporary sailing vessels: Amerigo Vespucci, Clearwater, Constitution, Eagle, Mayflower, Sea Cloud, Victory, many more. Authoritative captions provide statistics, background on each ship. 190 black-and-white photographs and illustrations. Introduction. 128pp. 8⅞ x 11¾. 27163-3 Pa. $13.95

EARLY NINETEENTH-CENTURY CRAFTS AND TRADES, Peter Stockham (ed.). Extremely rare 1807 volume describes to youngsters the crafts and trades of the day: brickmaker, weaver, dressmaker, bookbinder, ropemaker, saddler, many more. Quaint prose, charming illustrations for each craft. 20 black-and-white line illustrations. 192pp. 4⅝ x 6. 27293-1 Pa. $4.95

VICTORIAN FASHIONS AND COSTUMES FROM HARPER'S BAZAR, 1867–1898, Stella Blum (ed.). Day costumes, evening wear, sports clothes, shoes, hats, other accessories in over 1,000 detailed engravings. 320pp. 9⅜ x 12¼.
22990-4 Pa. $14.95

GUSTAV STICKLEY, THE CRAFTSMAN, Mary Ann Smith. Superb study surveys broad scope of Stickley's achievement, especially in architecture. Design philosophy, rise and fall of the Craftsman empire, descriptions and floor plans for many Craftsman houses, more. 86 black-and-white halftones. 31 line illustrations. Introduction 208pp. 6½ x 9¼. 27210-9 Pa. $9.95

THE LONG ISLAND RAIL ROAD IN EARLY PHOTOGRAPHS, Ron Ziel. Over 220 rare photos, informative text document origin (1844) and development of rail service on Long Island. Vintage views of early trains, locomotives, stations, passengers, crews, much more. Captions. 8⅞ x 11¾. 26301-0 Pa. $13.95

THE BOOK OF OLD SHIPS: From Egyptian Galleys to Clipper Ships, Henry B. Culver. Superb, authoritative history of sailing vessels, with 80 magnificent line illustrations. Galley, bark, caravel, longship, whaler, many more. Detailed, informative text on each vessel by noted naval historian. Introduction. 256pp. 5⅜ x 8½.
27332-6 Pa. $7.95

TEN BOOKS ON ARCHITECTURE, Vitruvius. The most important book ever written on architecture. Early Roman aesthetics, technology, classical orders, site selection, all other aspects. Morgan translation. 331pp. 5⅜ x 8½. 20645-9 Pa. $8.95

THE HUMAN FIGURE IN MOTION, Eadweard Muybridge. More than 4,500 stopped-action photos, in action series, showing undraped men, women, children jumping, lying down, throwing, sitting, wrestling, carrying, etc. 390pp. 7⅞ x 10⅝.
20204-6 Clothbd. $25.95

TREES OF THE EASTERN AND CENTRAL UNITED STATES AND CANADA, William M. Harlow. Best one-volume guide to 140 trees. Full descriptions, woodlore, range, etc. Over 600 illustrations. Handy size. 288pp. 4½ x 6⅜.
20395-6 Pa. $6.95

SONGS OF WESTERN BIRDS, Dr. Donald J. Borror. Complete song and call repertoire of 60 western species, including flycatchers, juncoes, cactus wrens, many more–includes fully illustrated booklet. Cassette and manual 99913-0 $8.95

GROWING AND USING HERBS AND SPICES, Milo Miloradovich. Versatile handbook provides all the information needed for cultivation and use of all the herbs and spices available in North America. 4 illustrations. Index. Glossary. 236pp. 5⅜ x 8½.
25058-X Pa. $6.95

BIG BOOK OF MAZES AND LABYRINTHS, Walter Shepherd. 50 mazes and labyrinths in all–classical, solid, ripple, and more–in one great volume. Perfect inexpensive puzzler for clever youngsters. Full solutions. 112pp. 8⅛ x 11.
22951-3 Pa. $4.95

CATALOG OF DOVER BOOKS

PIANO TUNING, J. Cree Fischer. Clearest, best book for beginner, amateur. Simple repairs, raising dropped notes, tuning by easy method of flattened fifths. No previous skills needed. 4 illustrations. 201pp. 5⅜ x 8½. 23267-0 Pa. $6.95

A SOURCE BOOK IN THEATRICAL HISTORY, A. M. Nagler. Contemporary observers on acting, directing, make-up, costuming, stage props, machinery, scene design, from Ancient Greece to Chekhov. 611pp. 5⅜ x 8½. 20515-0 Pa. $12.95

THE COMPLETE NONSENSE OF EDWARD LEAR, Edward Lear. All nonsense limericks, zany alphabets, Owl and Pussycat, songs, nonsense botany, etc., illustrated by Lear. Total of 320pp. 5⅜ x 8½. (USO) 20167-8 Pa. $6.95

VICTORIAN PARLOUR POETRY: An Annotated Anthology, Michael R. Turner. 117 gems by Longfellow, Tennyson, Browning, many lesser-known poets. "The Village Blacksmith," "Curfew Must Not Ring Tonight," "Only a Baby Small," dozens more, often difficult to find elsewhere. Index of poets, titles, first lines. xxiii + 325pp. 5⅜ x 8¼. 27044-0 Pa. $8.95

DUBLINERS, James Joyce. Fifteen stories offer vivid, tightly focused observations of the lives of Dublin's poorer classes. At least one, "The Dead," is considered a masterpiece. Reprinted complete and unabridged from standard edition. 160pp. 5³⁄₁₆ x 8¼. 26870-5 Pa. $1.00

THE HAUNTED MONASTERY and THE CHINESE MAZE MURDERS, Robert van Gulik. Two full novels by van Gulik, set in 7th-century China, continue adventures of Judge Dee and his companions. An evil Taoist monastery, seemingly supernatural events; overgrown topiary maze hides strange crimes. 27 illustrations. 328pp. 5⅜ x 8½. 23502-5 Pa. $8.95

THE BOOK OF THE SACRED MAGIC OF ABRAMELIN THE MAGE, translated by S. MacGregor Mathers. Medieval manuscript of ceremonial magic. Basic document in Aleister Crowley, Golden Dawn groups. 268pp. 5⅜ x 8½. 23211-5 Pa. $8.95

NEW RUSSIAN-ENGLISH AND ENGLISH-RUSSIAN DICTIONARY, M. A. O'Brien. This is a remarkably handy Russian dictionary, containing a surprising amount of information, including over 70,000 entries. 366pp. 4½ x 6¼. 20208-9 Pa. $9.95

HISTORIC HOMES OF THE AMERICAN PRESIDENTS, Second, Revised Edition, Irvin Haas. A traveler's guide to American Presidential homes, most open to the public, depicting and describing homes occupied by every American President from George Washington to George Bush. With visiting hours, admission charges, travel routes. 175 photographs. Index. 160pp. 8¼ x 11. 26751-2 Pa. $11.95

NEW YORK IN THE FORTIES, Andreas Feininger. 162 brilliant photographs by the well-known photographer, formerly with *Life* magazine. Commuters, shoppers, Times Square at night, much else from city at its peak. Captions by John von Hartz. 181pp. 9¼ x 10¾. 23585-8 Pa. $12.95

INDIAN SIGN LANGUAGE, William Tomkins. Over 525 signs developed by Sioux and other tribes. Written instructions and diagrams. Also 290 pictographs. 111pp. 6⅛ x 9¼. 22029-X Pa. $3.95

ANATOMY: A Complete Guide for Artists, Joseph Sheppard. A master of figure drawing shows artists how to render human anatomy convincingly. Over 460 illustrations. 224pp. 8⅜ x 11¼. 27279-6 Pa. $10.95

MEDIEVAL CALLIGRAPHY: Its History and Technique, Marc Drogin. Spirited history, comprehensive instruction manual covers 13 styles (ca. 4th century thru 15th). Excellent photographs; directions for duplicating medieval techniques with modern tools. 224pp. 8⅜ x 11¼. 26142-5 Pa. $12.95

DRIED FLOWERS: How to Prepare Them, Sarah Whitlock and Martha Rankin. Complete instructions on how to use silica gel, meal and borax, perlite aggregate, sand and borax, glycerine and water to create attractive permanent flower arrangements. 12 illustrations. 32pp. 5⅜ x 8½. 21802-3 Pa. $1.00

EASY-TO-MAKE BIRD FEEDERS FOR WOODWORKERS, Scott D. Campbell. Detailed, simple-to-use guide for designing, constructing, caring for and using feeders. Text, illustrations for 12 classic and contemporary designs. 96pp. 5⅜ x 8½. 25847-5 Pa. $2.95

SCOTTISH WONDER TALES FROM MYTH AND LEGEND, Donald A. Mackenzie. 16 lively tales tell of giants rumbling down mountainsides, of a magic wand that turns stone pillars into warriors, of gods and goddesses, evil hags, powerful forces and more. 240pp. 5⅜ x 8½. 29677-6 Pa. $6.95

THE HISTORY OF UNDERCLOTHES, C. Willett Cunnington and Phyllis Cunnington. Fascinating, well-documented survey covering six centuries of English undergarments, enhanced with over 100 illustrations: 12th-century laced-up bodice, footed long drawers (1795), 19th-century bustles, 19th-century corsets for men, Victorian "bust improvers," much more. 272pp. 5⅝ x 8¼. 27124-2 Pa. $9.95

ARTS AND CRAFTS FURNITURE: The Complete Brooks Catalog of 1912, Brooks Manufacturing Co. Photos and detailed descriptions of more than 150 now very collectible furniture designs from the Arts and Crafts movement depict davenports, settees, buffets, desks, tables, chairs, bedsteads, dressers and more, all built of solid, quarter-sawed oak. Invaluable for students and enthusiasts of antiques, Americana and the decorative arts. 80pp. 6½ x 9¼. 27471-3 Pa. $8.95

HOW WE INVENTED THE AIRPLANE: An Illustrated History, Orville Wright. Fascinating firsthand account covers early experiments, construction of planes and motors, first flights, much more. Introduction and commentary by Fred C. Kelly. 76 photographs. 96pp. 8¼ x 11. 25662-6 Pa. $8.95

THE ARTS OF THE SAILOR: Knotting, Splicing and Ropework, Hervey Garrett Smith. Indispensable shipboard reference covers tools, basic knots and useful hitches; handsewing and canvas work, more. Over 100 illustrations. Delightful reading for sea lovers. 256pp. 5⅜ x 8½. 26440-8 Pa. $7.95

FRANK LLOYD WRIGHT'S FALLINGWATER: The House and Its History, Second, Revised Edition, Donald Hoffmann. A total revision–both in text and illustrations–of the standard document on Fallingwater, the boldest, most personal architectural statement of Wright's mature years, updated with valuable new material from the recently opened Frank Lloyd Wright Archives. "Fascinating"–*The New York Times*. 116 illustrations. 128pp. 9¼ x 10¾. 27430-6 Pa. $11.95

PHOTOGRAPHIC SKETCHBOOK OF THE CIVIL WAR, Alexander Gardner. 100 photos taken on field during the Civil War. Famous shots of Manassas Harper's Ferry, Lincoln, Richmond, slave pens, etc. 244pp. 10⅝ x 8¼.   22731-6 Pa. $9.95

FIVE ACRES AND INDEPENDENCE, Maurice G. Kains. Great back-to-the-land classic explains basics of self-sufficient farming. The one book to get. 95 illustrations. 397pp. 5⅜ x 8½.   20974-1 Pa. $7.95

SONGS OF EASTERN BIRDS, Dr. Donald J. Borror. Songs and calls of 60 species most common to eastern U.S.: warblers, woodpeckers, flycatchers, thrushes, larks, many more in high-quality recording.   Cassette and manual 99912-2 $9.95

A MODERN HERBAL, Margaret Grieve. Much the fullest, most exact, most useful compilation of herbal material. Gigantic alphabetical encyclopedia, from aconite to zedoary, gives botanical information, medical properties, folklore, economic uses, much else. Indispensable to serious reader. 161 illustrations. 888pp. 6½ x 9¼. 2-vol. set. (USO)   Vol. I: 22798-7 Pa. $9.95
Vol. II: 22799-5 Pa. $9.95

HIDDEN TREASURE MAZE BOOK, Dave Phillips. Solve 34 challenging mazes accompanied by heroic tales of adventure. Evil dragons, people-eating plants, blood-thirsty giants, many more dangerous adversaries lurk at every twist and turn. 34 mazes, stories, solutions. 48pp. 8¼ x 11.   24566-7 Pa. $2.95

LETTERS OF W. A. MOZART, Wolfgang A. Mozart. Remarkable letters show bawdy wit, humor, imagination, musical insights, contemporary musical world; includes some letters from Leopold Mozart. 276pp. 5⅜ x 8½.   22859-2 Pa. $7.95

BASIC PRINCIPLES OF CLASSICAL BALLET, Agrippina Vaganova. Great Russian theoretician, teacher explains methods for teaching classical ballet. 118 illustrations. 175pp. 5⅜ x 8½.   22036-2 Pa. $5.95

THE JUMPING FROG, Mark Twain. Revenge edition. The original story of The Celebrated Jumping Frog of Calaveras County, a hapless French translation, and Twain's hilarious "retranslation" from the French. 12 illustrations. 66pp. 5⅜ x 8½.   22686-7 Pa. $3.95

BEST REMEMBERED POEMS, Martin Gardner (ed.). The 126 poems in this superb collection of 19th- and 20th-century British and American verse range from Shelley's "To a Skylark" to the impassioned "Renascence" of Edna St. Vincent Millay and to Edward Lear's whimsical "The Owl and the Pussycat." 224pp. 5⅜ x 8½.   27165-X Pa. $4.95

COMPLETE SONNETS, William Shakespeare. Over 150 exquisite poems deal with love, friendship, the tyranny of time, beauty's evanescence, death and other themes in language of remarkable power, precision and beauty. Glossary of archaic terms. 80pp. 5³⁄₁₆ x 8¼.   26686-9 Pa. $1.00

BODIES IN A BOOKSHOP, R. T. Campbell. Challenging mystery of blackmail and murder with ingenious plot and superbly drawn characters. In the best tradition of British suspense fiction. 192pp. 5⅜ x 8½.   24720-1 Pa. $6.95

THE WIT AND HUMOR OF OSCAR WILDE, Alvin Redman (ed.). More than 1,000 ripostes, paradoxes, wisecracks: Work is the curse of the drinking classes; I can resist everything except temptation; etc. 258pp. 5⅜ x 8½. 20602-5 Pa. $5.95

SHAKESPEARE LEXICON AND QUOTATION DICTIONARY, Alexander Schmidt. Full definitions, locations, shades of meaning in every word in plays and poems. More than 50,000 exact quotations. 1,485pp. 6½ x 9¼. 2-vol. set.
Vol. 1: 22726-X Pa. $16.95
Vol. 2: 22727-8 Pa. $16.95

SELECTED POEMS, Emily Dickinson. Over 100 best-known, best-loved poems by one of America's foremost poets, reprinted from authoritative early editions. No comparable edition at this price. Index of first lines. 64pp. 5 3/16 x 8¼.
26466-1 Pa. $1.00

CELEBRATED CASES OF JUDGE DEE (DEE GOONG AN), translated by Robert van Gulik. Authentic 18th-century Chinese detective novel; Dee and associates solve three interlocked cases. Led to van Gulik's own stories with same characters. Extensive introduction. 9 illustrations. 237pp. 5⅜ x 8½. 23337-5 Pa. $6.95

THE MALLEUS MALEFICARUM OF KRAMER AND SPRENGER, translated by Montague Summers. Full text of most important witchhunter's "bible," used by both Catholics and Protestants. 278pp. 6⅝ x 10. 22802-9 Pa. $12.95

SPANISH STORIES/CUENTOS ESPAÑOLES: A Dual-Language Book, Angel Flores (ed.). Unique format offers 13 great stories in Spanish by Cervantes, Borges, others. Faithful English translations on facing pages. 352pp. 5⅜ x 8½.
25399-6 Pa. $8.95

THE CHICAGO WORLD'S FAIR OF 1893: A Photographic Record, Stanley Appelbaum (ed.). 128 rare photos show 200 buildings, Beaux-Arts architecture, Midway, original Ferris Wheel, Edison's kinetoscope, more. Architectural emphasis; full text. 116pp. 8¼ x 11. 23990-X Pa. $9.95

OLD QUEENS, N.Y., IN EARLY PHOTOGRAPHS, Vincent F. Seyfried and William Asadorian. Over 160 rare photographs of Maspeth, Jamaica, Jackson Heights, and other areas. Vintage views of DeWitt Clinton mansion, 1939 World's Fair and more. Captions. 192pp. 8⅞ x 11. 26358-4 Pa. $12.95

CAPTURED BY THE INDIANS: 15 Firsthand Accounts, 1750-1870, Frederick Drimmer. Astounding true historical accounts of grisly torture, bloody conflicts, relentless pursuits, miraculous escapes and more, by people who lived to tell the tale. 384pp. 5⅜ x 8½. 24901-8 Pa. $8.95

THE WORLD'S GREAT SPEECHES, Lewis Copeland and Lawrence W. Lamm (eds.). Vast collection of 278 speeches of Greeks to 1970. Powerful and effective models; unique look at history. 842pp. 5⅜ x 8½. 20468-5 Pa. $14.95

THE BOOK OF THE SWORD, Sir Richard F. Burton. Great Victorian scholar/adventurer's eloquent, erudite history of the "queen of weapons"—from prehistory to early Roman Empire. Evolution and development of early swords, variations (sabre, broadsword, cutlass, scimitar, etc.), much more. 336pp. 6⅛ x 9¼.
25434-8 Pa. $9.95

AUTOBIOGRAPHY: The Story of My Experiments with Truth, Mohandas K. Gandhi. Boyhood, legal studies, purification, the growth of the Satyagraha (nonviolent protest) movement. Critical, inspiring work of the man responsible for the freedom of India. 480pp. 5⅜ x 8½. (USO)   24593-4 Pa. $8.95

CELTIC MYTHS AND LEGENDS, T. W. Rolleston. Masterful retelling of Irish and Welsh stories and tales. Cuchulain, King Arthur, Deirdre, the Grail, many more. First paperback edition. 58 full-page illustrations. 512pp. 5⅜ x 8½.   26507-2 Pa. $9.95

THE PRINCIPLES OF PSYCHOLOGY, William James. Famous long course complete, unabridged. Stream of thought, time perception, memory, experimental methods; great work decades ahead of its time. 94 figures. 1,391pp. 5⅜ x 8½. 2-vol. set.
Vol. I: 20381-6 Pa. $12.95
Vol. II: 20382-4 Pa. $12.95

THE WORLD AS WILL AND REPRESENTATION, Arthur Schopenhauer. Definitive English translation of Schopenhauer's life work, correcting more than 1,000 errors, omissions in earlier translations. Translated by E. F. J. Payne. Total of 1,269pp. 5⅜ x 8½. 2-vol. set.
Vol. 1: 21761-2 Pa. $11.95
Vol. 2: 21762-0 Pa. $12.95

MAGIC AND MYSTERY IN TIBET, Madame Alexandra David-Neel. Experiences among lamas, magicians, sages, sorcerers, Bonpa wizards. A true psychic discovery. 32 illustrations. 321pp. 5⅜ x 8½. (USO)   22682-4 Pa. $8.95

THE EGYPTIAN BOOK OF THE DEAD, E. A. Wallis Budge. Complete reproduction of Ani's papyrus, finest ever found. Full hieroglyphic text, interlinear transliteration, word-for-word translation, smooth translation. 533pp. 6½ x 9¼.
21866-X Pa. $10.95

MATHEMATICS FOR THE NONMATHEMATICIAN, Morris Kline. Detailed, college-level treatment of mathematics in cultural and historical context, with numerous exercises. Recommended Reading Lists. Tables. Numerous figures. 641pp. 5⅜ x 8½.
24823-2 Pa. $11.95

THEORY OF WING SECTIONS: Including a Summary of Airfoil Data, Ira H. Abbott and A. E. von Doenhoff. Concise compilation of subsonic aerodynamic characteristics of NACA wing sections, plus description of theory. 350pp. of tables. 693pp. 5⅜ x 8½.   60586-8 Pa. $14.95

THE RIME OF THE ANCIENT MARINER, Gustave Doré, S. T. Coleridge. Doré's finest work; 34 plates capture moods, subtleties of poem. Flawless full-size reproductions printed on facing pages with authoritative text of poem. "Beautiful. Simply beautiful."—Publisher's Weekly. 77pp. 9¼ x 12.   22305-1 Pa. $6.95

NORTH AMERICAN INDIAN DESIGNS FOR ARTISTS AND CRAFTSPEOPLE, Eva Wilson. Over 360 authentic copyright-free designs adapted from Navajo blankets, Hopi pottery, Sioux buffalo hides, more. Geometrics, symbolic figures, plant and animal motifs, etc. 128pp. 8⅜ x 11. (EUK)   25341-4 Pa. $8.95

SCULPTURE: Principles and Practice, Louis Slobodkin. Step-by-step approach to clay, plaster, metals, stone; classical and modern. 253 drawings, photos. 255pp. 8⅛ x 11.
22960-2 Pa. $11.95

CATALOG OF DOVER BOOKS

THE INFLUENCE OF SEA POWER UPON HISTORY, 1660–1783, A. T. Mahan. Influential classic of naval history and tactics still used as text in war colleges. First paperback edition. 4 maps. 24 battle plans. 640pp. 5⅜ x 8½. 25509-3 Pa. $12.95

THE STORY OF THE TITANIC AS TOLD BY ITS SURVIVORS, Jack Winocour (ed.). What it was really like. Panic, despair, shocking inefficiency, and a little heroism. More thrilling than any fictional account. 26 illustrations. 320pp. 5⅜ x 8½. 20610-6 Pa. $8.95

FAIRY AND FOLK TALES OF THE IRISH PEASANTRY, William Butler Yeats (ed.). Treasury of 64 tales from the twilight world of Celtic myth and legend: "The Soul Cages," "The Kildare Pooka," "King O'Toole and his Goose," many more. Introduction and Notes by W. B. Yeats. 352pp. 5⅜ x 8½. 26941-8 Pa. $8.95

BUDDHIST MAHAYANA TEXTS, E. B. Cowell and Others (eds.). Superb, accurate translations of basic documents in Mahayana Buddhism, highly important in history of religions. The Buddha-karita of Asvaghosha, Larger Sukhavativyuha, more. 448pp. 5⅜ x 8½. 25552-2 Pa. $12.95

ONE TWO THREE . . . INFINITY: Facts and Speculations of Science, George Gamow. Great physicist's fascinating, readable overview of contemporary science: number theory, relativity, fourth dimension, entropy, genes, atomic structure, much more. 128 illustrations. Index. 352pp. 5⅜ x 8½. 25664-2 Pa. $8.95

ENGINEERING IN HISTORY, Richard Shelton Kirby, et al. Broad, nontechnical survey of history's major technological advances: birth of Greek science, industrial revolution, electricity and applied science, 20th-century automation, much more. 181 illustrations. ". . . excellent . . ."–*Isis*. Bibliography. vii + 530pp. 5⅜ x 8¼. 26412-2 Pa. $14.95

DALÍ ON MODERN ART: The Cuckolds of Antiquated Modern Art, Salvador Dalí. Influential painter skewers modern art and its practitioners. Outrageous evaluations of Picasso, Cézanne, Turner, more. 15 renderings of paintings discussed. 44 calligraphic decorations by Dalí. 96pp. 5⅜ x 8½. (USO) 29220-7 Pa. $4.95

ANTIQUE PLAYING CARDS: A Pictorial History, Henry René D'Allemagne. Over 900 elaborate, decorative images from rare playing cards (14th–20th centuries): Bacchus, death, dancing dogs, hunting scenes, royal coats of arms, players cheating, much more. 96pp. 9¼ x 12¼. 29265-7 Pa. $11.95

MAKING FURNITURE MASTERPIECES: 30 Projects with Measured Drawings, Franklin H. Gottshall. Step-by-step instructions, illustrations for constructing handsome, useful pieces, among them a Sheraton desk, Chippendale chair, Spanish desk, Queen Anne table and a William and Mary dressing mirror. 224pp. 8⅛ x 11¼. 29338-6 Pa. $13.95

THE FOSSIL BOOK: A Record of Prehistoric Life, Patricia V. Rich et al. Profusely illustrated definitive guide covers everything from single-celled organisms and dinosaurs to birds and mammals and the interplay between climate and man. Over 1,500 illustrations. 760pp. 7½ x 10⅛. 29371-8 Pa. $29.95

Prices subject to change without notice.

Available at your book dealer or write for free catalog to Dept. GI, Dover Publications, Inc., 31 East 2nd St., Mineola, N.Y. 11501. Dover publishes more than 500 books each year on science, elementary and advanced mathematics, biology, music, art, literary history, social sciences and other areas.